GUINNESS WORLD RECORDS

OUTRAGEOUS!

FUN FACTS & ACTIVITIES

AMERICAN
EDUCATION
PUBLISHING™

American Education Publishing™
An imprint of Carson-Dellosa Publishing LLC
Greensboro, North Carolina

Photo: Guinness World Records Limited

Photo: Guinness World Records Limited

WHAT'S INSIDE?

Photo: Guinness World Records Limited

CAUTION   CAUTION   CAUTION

A Note to the Reader of This Book

Inside this book, you will find facts about unusual objects and creatures, epic journeys, and thrilling feats. Read and enjoy the stories, but never try to set a world record on your own! Breaking records can be dangerous and even life threatening. If you think you have a good idea for a safe, record-breaking event, talk to an adult. You can learn more about how to set a world record at guinnessworldrecords.com.

Throughout this book, you will find activity ideas that encourage you to learn more, get active, use your brain, be creative, and have fun. Try all the activities, but pause and think before you do each one. Ask yourself: What should I do to be safe and follow the rules? Do I need a parent's permission to go somewhere or to use materials? Always ask an adult if you are unsure.

Now, turn to any page. Get ready to be amazed by Guinness World Records® facts!

CAUTION   CAUTION   CAUTION

Photo: Image used under license from Shutterstock.com

MAGNIFICENT EARTH

Photo: ©2000 Photodisc, Inc.

Worst Cyclone Disaster (Damage Toll)

Photo: Image used under license from Shutterstock.com

Hurricane Katrina devastated the coast of Louisiana during the 2005 hurricane season. The damage total reached an estimated $100 billion.

Did You Know?

Since 1953, hurricanes have been named by the National Hurricane Center. Boys' names alternate with girls' names. The lists repeat every six years.

ACTIVITIES

1. The root *cycl* means "circle." Some words with *cycl* are *cycle* and *bicycle*. Explain how *cyclone* fits with these words.

_____

2. List things that move in a circle.

_____   _____

_____   _____

3. Hurricane Katrina hit the U.S. in 2005. How many years ago was that?

_____

Largest Haystack

De hoogste hooibult ter wereld
30 jaar Flaeijelfeest
28 t/m 30 september 2006

Photo: Guinness World Records Limited

On July 6, 2006, in Friesland, Netherlands, the largest haystack measured 31 ft. 2 in. (9.51 m) tall and had a diameter of 55 ft. 9 in. (17 m).

Did You Know?

If someone says "it's like looking for a needle in a haystack," it means it's going to be very difficult to find.

ACTIVITIES

1. Livestock eat hay, especially in the winter. What are your favorite farm animals that eat hay?

   _____

2. Each story, or level, of a building is about 10 feet tall. About how many stories tall is the largest haystack?

   _____

3. What does it mean to say, "I need to hit the hay"?

   _____

Highest Text Message

Photo: Guinness World Records Limited

On May 21, 2007, Rod Baber (UK) successfully sent a text message from an altitude of 29,029 ft. (8,848 m) on the summit of Mt. Everest, Nepal. The text message read, "One small step for man one giant step for mobilekind—thanks Motorola."

Did You Know?

The first text message ever was sent in December 1992. It read, "Merry Christmas."

ACTIVITIES

1. A *character* is a letter or symbol typed on a keyboard. Text messages are usually limited to 160 characters. Write a message to a friend that is exactly 160 characters long.

   _____

   _____

2. Write this text message in sentences: don't B L8 4 parT 2night C U soon.

   _____

   _____

Heaviest Watermelon

Photo: Guinness World Records Limited

Lloyd Bright (USA) presented a watermelon weighing 268.8 lb. (121.93 kg) at the annual Big Watermelon Contest in Hope, Arkansas, on September 3, 2005.

Did You Know?
Some early explorers used watermelons as canteens!

ACTIVITIES

1. A nine-year-old human weighs about 65 pounds. About how many nine-year-olds would it take to equal the weight of the heaviest watermelon?

   _____

2. Use these word parts to write the names of four fruits: *blue, melon, water, apple, pine, berry, straw.*

   _____   _____

   _____   _____

First Men on the Moon

Photo: ©NASA

On July 20, 1969, Neil Alden Armstrong (USA) became the first man to set foot on the moon. He was followed out of the lunar module by Edwin Eugene "Buzz" Aldrin, Jr. (USA).

Did You Know?

Because there is no wind to blow them away, Neil Armstrong's footprints will remain on the surface of the moon for at least a million years.

CHECK THIS OUT!

On July 20, 1969, Neil Armstrong (United States) became the first person to walk on the moon. Minutes later, he was followed by Edwin Eugene "Buzz" Aldrin, Jr. (United States). The two men stepped out of a lunar landing vehicle named the *Eagle*. They were part of a United States mission to put a man on the moon. The mission was called *Apollo 11*.

The *Apollo 11* spacecraft blasted off from Florida with three men aboard. It took them five days to reach the moon. Then, Armstrong and Aldrin left the main spacecraft, taking the *Eagle* down to the surface of the moon. Back on Earth, people watched on TV as Armstrong took his first step. "That's one small step for man, one giant leap for mankind," he said.

1. Three men from *Apollo 11* walked on the moon. True or false?
   Circle your answer.

   true   **false**

2. In Latin, the word for "sun" is *sol*. That is why *solar* means "something that
   relates to the sun." In Latin, the word for "moon" is *luna*. So, what do you
   think *lunar* means?

   _____

3. Do you think the *Eagle* was a good name for the lunar landing vehicle?
   Explain why or why not.

   _____

   _____

4. Circle five words you read on page 10 to complete the word search. Use the word
   bank to help you.

   Buzz   Eagle   Apollo   Florida   Neil

B	U	Z	Z	E	G	L
R	A	U	H	A	J	S
B	P	I	J	G	O	Z
N	O	L	S	L	E	C
A	L	P	N	E	I	L
F	L	O	R	I	D	A
E	O	Q	Y	U	I	V

Greatest Rainfall in 24 Hours

Photo: Image used under license from Shutterstock.com

About 16.6 million lb. (7,554 metric tons) of rain per acre fell on Reunion Island in the Indian Ocean between March 15 and 16, 1952, for a total of 73 in. (1.85 m) of rainfall.

Did You Know?

Raindrops at night can make a lunar rainbow, or moonbow. Moonbows are just moonlit rainbows that appear at night.

ACTIVITIES

1. What is the average annual rainfall in inches for your city? Do some research to find out.

   _____

2. Write what you like to do on a rainy day.

   _____

3. Rain is one type of precipitation. Name two more types.

   _____   _____

Largest Sand Painting

Photo: Guinness World Records Limited

On January 26, 2009, Dr. Pranali Patidar and 150 college students in Dhule, India, created a sand painting that measured 64,583.5 sq. ft. (6,000 m²)

Did You Know?

There are about 250,000 grains of sand in a 3-minute hourglass.

ACTIVITIES

1. Would you rather complete an art project by yourself or with a group of friends? Explain your answer.

   _____

2. With adult help, color salt or sugar with food coloring. Sprinkle some on glue to make a painting. Write what you did.

   _____

3. With a friend, display artwork you have done. Label each piece and invite guests. Name your gallery.

   _____

Greatest Mountain Range on Earth

Photo: Image used under license from Shutterstock.com

The Himalayas were formed between 30 and 50 million years ago. They contain nine of the 10 tallest peaks, including Mount Everest, the tallest mountain in the world.

Did You Know?
About 4,000 people have tried to climb to Mt. Everest's peak. Only 660 have made it so far.

ACTIVITIES

1. What mountain range is nearest to your home?

   _____

2. Would you rather climb a mountain or explore a cave? Why?

   _____

3. Mt. Everest is 29,029 feet tall. The second tallest mountain, called *K2*, is 28,251 feet tall. How many feet taller is Mt. Everest?

   _____

Heaviest Avocado

Photo: Guinness World Records Limited

Gabriel Ramirez Nahim (Venezuela) presented an avocado that weighed 4 lb. 13 oz. (2.19 kg) on January 28, 2009.

Did You Know?

Another name for the avocado is the *Alligator Pear*, because of its shape and its green skin.

ACTIVITIES

1. Avocados are the main ingredient in guacamole. What words can you make from the letters G-U-A-C-A-M-O-L-E?

_____   _____   _____

_____   _____   _____

2. A California avocado tree can produce 500 avocados each year. How much could one tree produce in 4.5 years?

_____

Tallest Snowman

Photo: Guinness World Records Limited

The residents of Bethel, Maine, and surrounding towns built a snowman that stood 122 ft. 1 in. (37.21 m) tall. It took one month to build and was completed on February 26, 2008.

Did You Know?

This snowman was actually a snowwoman named Olympia. She weighed 13,000,000 lb. (5,896,701 kg) and didn't completely melt until July 30, 2008.

CHECK THIS OUT!

If you live where it snows, you have probably built a snowman. The people of Bethel, Maine, know all about building snowmen. In 1999, the people in this town built the tallest snowman ever, and nine years later, they made an even bigger one!

The new snowman was called *Olympia*, so it was actually a snowwoman! It took the town about a month to finish making her, with everyone pitching in to help. Children had the job of painting her nose orange. To make her lips, five car tires were painted bright red. Her eyes were made from five-foot wreaths. Her eyelashes came from 16 old skis. Olympia had three truck tires for buttons and a 130-foot scarf. Two thousand feet of yellow rope was used for hair.

ACTIVITIES

1. Why do you think Olympia took until July 30 to melt completely?

_____

2. Draw a picture of what you think Olympia looked like as she started to melt.

3. What are eight adjectives you could use to describe Olympia?

_____   _____

_____   _____

_____   _____

_____   _____

4. Imagine you are building a snowman the size of Olympia. What supplies would you need?

_____

_____

5. One ton is equal to 2,000 pounds. Olympia weighed 13,000,000 pounds. How many tons is that? Research to find out how much a typical car weighs. Did Olympia weigh more or less than a car?

_____

Most Tornadoes in 24 Hours

A record 148 tornadoes swept through the southern and mid-western United States on April 3–4, 1974. This region of America is often referred to as "Tornado Alley."

Did You Know?
Tornado winds are strong enough to drive a piece of straw into a tree.

Photo: Image used under license from Shutterstock.com

ACTIVITIES

1. About 800 tornadoes are spotted each year in the U.S. When did a tornado last happen in your state? Research to find out.

_____

2. Make a tornado with a two-liter bottle. Fill it with water and go outside. Turn the bottle upside down, covering the hole with your hand. Swish the water to get it moving in a circular direction. Remove your hand and let the water pour out. What did you see?

_____

_____

Largest Stone Sculpture

Photo: Guinness World Records Limited

In the Meng Shan Mountains near Pingyi, Shandong, China, the largest stone sculpture is carved into the northwest side of the peak. It measures 715 ft. (218 m) high and 656 ft. (200 m) wide and can be seen from 12 to 19 mi. (20 to 30 km) away.

Did You Know?

The four U.S. presidents' heads carved in rocks at Mount Rushmore are expected to erode about 1 in. (2.54 cm) every 10,000 years.

ACTIVITIES

1. The Largest Stone Sculpture can be seen from 12-19 miles away. Could you see it from 18 miles away? Circle your answer.

   yes   **maybe**   **no**

2. What image would you carve into the side of a mountain? How would you want people to feel when they saw it?

   _____

3. What four U.S. presidents can be seen at Mount Rushmore?

   _____   _____

   _____   _____

Heaviest Jackfruit

Photo: Guinness World Records Limited

On August 8, 2003, George and Margaret Schattauer (both USA) presented a jackfruit that measured 22.62 in. (57.46 cm) long and had a circumference of 47.75 in. (121.28 cm). It weighed 76 lb. 4.4 oz. (34.6 kg).

Did You Know?

An unopened, ripe jackfruit smells like rotten onions. But open it up and it smells delicious—like pineapple and banana.

ACTIVITIES

1. The heaviest jackfruit weighed about 76 pounds. Do you weigh more or less than the jackfruit? Circle your answer.

   more   **less**

2. Jackfruit is used in Asian foods. It tastes like banana and is good with coconut, honey, sugar, and milk. What toppings would you put on an ice cream and jackfruit sundae?

   _____

3. What fruit is grown in your area?

   _____

Largest Ice Maze

Photo: Guinness World Records Limited

The Arctic Glacier Ice Maze in Buffalo, New York, was measured on February 26, 2010, and has an area of 12,855.68 sq. ft. (1,194.33 m²). The walls measure 6 ft. (1.83 m) high.

Did You Know?

About 50 volunteers built this maze by putting together 2,171 blocks of ice that weighed 300 lb. (136 kg) each.

ACTIVITIES

1. The ice maze walls are six feet tall. If you stood on a stool that was $10\frac{1}{2}$ inches high, could you see over the walls? Circle your answer.

    yes   no

2. Draw a maze in the space below. Ask a friend to solve it.

Largest Cut Diamond

An unnamed fancy black diamond, containing small red diamond crystals, weighs 555.55 carats. It was polished into 55 facets over several years and was completed in June 2004.

Did You Know?

Diamonds are made of the same material as the point in your pencil.

Photo: Guinness World Records Limited

CHECK THIS OUT!

Diamonds are known for their sparkle. When first found, a diamond looks like a plain stone. It takes trained people with special tools to make diamonds shine. These people cut flat surfaces, or facets, on the stones. The angles of the facets make the gem reflect light. The world's Largest Cut Diamond is black, has 55 facets, and weighs 555.55 carats. A *carat* is the measurement of a gem's weight. The largest diamond is about the size of a chicken egg!

On the other end of the scale, the world's Smallest Brilliant Cut Diamond is about the size of a grain of sand! It has 57 facets. Pauline Willemse (Netherlands), who cut the stone, worked on the diamond from 1991 to 1994.

ACTIVITIES

1. Which of the following words express the weight of the black diamond?

   a. fifty-five thousand five hundred fifty-five

   b. five hundred fifty-five and fifty-five hundredths

   c. five hundred fifty-five and fifty-five tenths

   d. fifty-five hundred and fifty-five hundredths

2. How many more facets does the world's Smallest Brilliant Cut Diamond have than the world's Largest Cut Diamond?

   _____

3. The gem cutter worked on the world's Smallest Brilliant Cut Diamond for _____ years.

   a. 3

   b. 5

   c. 10

   d. 13

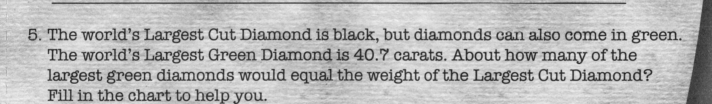

4. People often wear diamonds in jewelry, such as rings or earrings. Do you own a special piece of jewelry? Why is it meaningful to you?

   _____

   _____

5. The world's Largest Cut Diamond is black, but diamonds can also come in green. The world's Largest Green Diamond is 40.7 carats. About how many of the largest green diamonds would equal the weight of the Largest Cut Diamond? Fill in the chart to help you.

No. of Green Diamonds	1	2	3	4	5	6	7	8	9	10	11	12	13	14
Weight in Carats	40.7													

Number of Green Diamonds: _____

Fastest Crossing of the Atlantic by Solar Power

Photo: Guinness World Records Limited

The *sun21* (Switzerland) and its five-member crew crossed the Atlantic Ocean in 29 days. The voyage between one of the Canary Islands and Martinique began on January 4, 2007, and ended on February 2, 2007.

Did You Know?

In 1990, a solar-powered airplane flew across the United States on a 21-stop tour. Solar power can also heat swimming pools, cook food, and power cars.

ACTIVITIES

1. Name a machine you use every day that could be powered by solar energy.

2. Using conventional fuels, a boat can cross the Atlantic in just a few days and a plane can cross in a few hours. Is it worth the extra time to use solar power? Explain why or why not.

Largest Amethyst Geode

Photo: Guinness World Records Limited

The Shandong Tianyu Museum of Natural History (China) houses an amethyst geode that measures 9 ft. 10 in. (3 m) long, 5 ft. 10 in. (1.8 m) wide, 7 ft. 2 in. (2.2 m) high, and weighs 28,660 lb. (13 metric tons).

Did You Know?

Some people believe that if you put an amethyst under your pillow, it can help you understand your dreams!

ACTIVITIES

1. A geode looks like an ordinary rock, but reveals sparkling crystals when you crack it. What else can you break open to find good things inside?

_____   _____

_____   _____

2. The largest geode is about 10 feet long. Is that shorter or longer than the room you are in right now? Circle your answer.

shorter   longer

Slowest Flowering Plant

Photo: ©Luiz Claudio Marigo/naturepl.com

The giant bromeliad was discovered in the Bolivian mountains in 1870. Its flower cluster emerges after about 80 to 150 years of the plant's life. Once it has blossomed, the plant dies.

Did You Know?
This plant is part of the pineapple family. When it blooms, as many as 8,000 flowers may open on a single spike.

ACTIVITIES

1. Giant bromeliads take about 115 years to bloom. If one is planted today, in what year is it likely to bloom?

_____

2. On average, humans live for about 78 years. Do giant bromeliads have longer or shorter lives than humans? Circle your answer.

shorter   **longer**

3. What is your favorite plant or flower?

_____

Heaviest Hailstones

Photo: Courtesy NOAA

On April 14, 1986, a hailstone weighing 2 lb. 3 oz. (1 kg) fell in Bangladesh.

Did You Know?

In 1882, a hailstone with two frogs inside fell in Iowa. When the ice melted, the frogs hopped away!

ACTIVITIES

1. What weighs about two pounds? Use a bathroom scale to find out.

   _____

2. Hail forms only during thunderstorms. Tall, dense, mushroom-shaped cumulonimbus clouds bring thunderstorms with winds, rain, and lightning. Draw a thunderstorm.

Heaviest Lemon

Photo: Guinness World Records Limited

Aharon Shemoel (Israel) grew a lemon weighing 11 lb. 9.7 oz. (5.265 kg). It was 13.7 in. (35 cm) tall and had a circumference of 29 in. (74 cm) on January 8, 2003.

Did You Know?

Lemon trees bloom and produce fruit all year. A single tree can produce 500 to 600 lb. (227 to 272 kg) of lemons a year.

CHECK THIS OUT!

How big can a lemon get? The Heaviest Lemon ever grew to be the size of a large watermelon. At 11 pounds, 9.7 ounces, it weighed more than most newborn babies!

Lemons grow on trees like oranges and apples, but people do not eat them the same way. They are too sour. Lemons are used to flavor foods and make lemonade. Lemon juice is also a strong stain remover, and is an ingredient in soaps and lotions.

Lemon juice is rich in vitamin C. Mixed with water, lemon juice may help an upset stomach. It might also help relieve a high fever, a sore throat, or a headache. A lemon can be a very useful fruit!

ACTIVITIES

1. What does *ingredient* mean?

   _____

   _____

2. Name three ingredients in your favorite food.

   _____   _____   _____

3. Draw a picture to illustrate the expression, "When life gives you lemons, make lemonade."

4. In the passage on page 28, the word *relieve* means:

   a. strengthen

   b. identify

   c. help

   d. harm

5. Do you like the flavor of lemon? Explain why or why not.

   _____

6. Make your own recipe for lemonade. How many lemons would you use? How much water and sugar? Share your lemonade with your family. Do they like it?

   Lemons: _____   Water: _____   Sugar: _____

Highest Waterfall

Photo: Image used under license from Shutterstock.com

Angel Falls has a total drop of 3,212 ft. (979 m). It is located on a branch of the Carrao River, Venezuela. Locally, the waterfall is known as *Churun Meru*.

Did You Know?
Angel Falls is more than 12 times the height of Niagara Falls!

ACTIVITIES

1. There are 5,280 feet in a mile. Is the drop at Angel Falls shorter or longer than one mile? Circle your answer.

   shorter   **longer**

2. Imagine you are a rock tumbling over Angel Falls. Describe your experience.

   _____

   _____

   _____

Largest Sinosauropteryx Fossil

Photo: Guinness World Records Limited

The Shandong Tianyu Natural History Museum (China) houses a Sinosauropteryx fossil measuring 12 ft. 5 in. (3.8 m) long. The skull alone measures 1 ft. 11 in. (60 cm) long.

Did You Know?

The name *Sinosauropteryx* means "Chinese lizard wing." Scientists believe the creature may have had orange feathers and a striped tail.

ACTIVITIES

1. Many dinosaurs have *saur* (meaning "lizard") in their names. That's because scientists once thought dinosaurs were like lizards, even though they may have more in common with birds. Circle *saur* in each dinosaur name.

   Sinosauropteryx   **Allosaurus**

   Stegosaurus   **Tyrannosaurus rex**

2. Find objects from nature like rocks and shells. Press them into clay to make "fossils." Write what you see.

Most People Making Snow Angels Simultaneously

Photo: Guinness World Records Limited

In Bismarck, North Dakota, 8,962 people simultaneously made snow angels at the State Capitol Grounds on February 17, 2007.

Did You Know?

In 2008, an NFL football player was given a 15-yard penalty for making a snow angel just beyond the end line after his touchdown.

ACTIVITIES

1. The word *simultaneously* means "at the same time." With a friend, do a series of three things simultaneously. Try jumping, spinning, and touching your toes. Tell what you did. Was it easy or difficult?

_____

_____

2. Besides snow angels, what other shapes and patterns do humans and animals make in snow, mud, or sand?

_____

Largest Turquoise

Photo: Guinness World Records Limited

The Shandong Tianyu Museum of Natural History in Shandong Province, China, houses a turquoise that measures 3 ft. 5 in. (1.03 m) long, 3 ft. 6 in. (1.06 m) high, 10 in. (26 cm) wide, and weighs 496 lb. (225 kg).

Did You Know?
Some ancient Persians wore turquoise around their necks to ward off danger.

ACTIVITIES

1. The Largest Turquoise is three feet, six inches tall. Is the stone taller or shorter than you are? Circle your answer.

   shorter   **taller**

2. Many people love turquoise for its sky-blue color. What is your favorite color? What stone is that color?

   _____

3. The Mohs scale of 1–10 measures hardness. Fingernails are a 2 on the scale. Turquoise is a 5. What material do you think is very hard?

   _____

Most Leaves on a Clover

An 18-leaf clover was discovered by Shigeo Obara (Japan) on May 25, 2002.

Photo: Guinness World Records Limited

Did You Know?
Legend has it that Abraham Lincoln always carried around a four-leaf clover, except on the night of his assassination.

CHECK THIS OUT!

A *clover* is a plant with heart-shaped leaves. Almost all clover plants have three leaves. It is rare to find one with four leaves. Some people think that finding a four-leaf clover is good luck. A man from Japan actually found a clover with 18 leaves!

According to an old belief, each leaf on a clover has its own meaning. The first leaf stands for faith. The second leaf represents hope. The third leaf stands for love, and the fourth leaf, of course, is for luck.

The idea that a clover can bring good luck goes back hundreds of years. In 1620, Sir John Melton wrote about it. He said that anyone finding a four-leaf clover would soon "find some good thing."

ACTIVITIES

1. Some people think that a four-leaf clover is a sign of _____ .

   a. love

   b. faith

   c. luck

   d. hope

2. Sir John Melton wrote about finding "some good thing." Write about some good thing that you have found.

   _____

   _____

3. Think about the meaning people have given to each leaf of a four-leaf clover: faith, hope, love, and luck. If you found a five-leaf clover, what meaning would you give the fifth leaf? Explain your answer.

   _____

   _____

4. An 18-leaf clover is about the size of how many four-leaf clovers put together?

   _____

5. The year 1620 was how many years ago?

   _____

6. Draw your own 18-leaf clover.

Heaviest Onion

John Sifford (UK) grew an onion that weighed 16.5 lb. (7.5 kg) on September 16, 2005.

Photo: Guinness World Records Limited

Did You Know?

The Vidalia onion is the official state vegetable of Georgia. President Jimmy Carter often gave them out as White House gifts during his presidency (1977–1981).

ACTIVITIES

1. What is the official vegetable, bird, or flower of your state?

_____

2. Circle vegetables you would like to eat in a tasty stir-fry.

onions	carrots	corn
broccoli	peppers	peas
zucchini	spinach	shallots

Driving to the Highest Altitude by Car

Photo: Guinness World Records Limited

Gonzalo Bravo and Eduardo Canales (both Chile) drove a car to an altitude of 21,942 ft. (6,688 m) on the slopes of the Ojos Del Salado Volcano in Atacama, Chile, on April 21, 2007.

Did You Know?

Volcanic eruptions can set off a tsunami, flash flood, earthquake, mudflow, or rock fall, and have even knocked down entire forests.

ACTIVITIES

1. Altitude measures elevation above sea level. What place have you visited that has a high altitude?

   _____

2. Chile is in South America. What continent do you live on?

   _____

3. With adult help, make a volcanic "eruption" by pouring one cup of vinegar over one tablespoon of baking soda. What happened?

   _____

Largest Ice Village

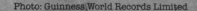

Photo: Guinness World Records Limited

In December 2002, the largest ice village was constructed to accommodate 700 guests near the famous Ice Hotel in Jukkasjärvi, Sweden. The village consisted of 140 huts. Each hut was 7 ft. (2.1 m) tall and had a diameter of 14 ft. (4.3 m).

Did You Know?
Guests at this famous Ice Hotel, rebuilt every winter, curl up inside sleeping bags on top of beds made of packed ice and snow.

ACTIVITIES

1. Would you like to sleep in a snow hut? Explain why or why not.

_____

2. The ice village had 140 huts for 700 guests. How many people stayed in each hut?

_____

3. Ice melts at 32°F. The average temperature in Sweden in April is 47°F. What happens to the ice village in April?

_____

Tallest Sunflower

Photo: Guinness World Records Limited

Hans-Peter Schiffer (Germany) presented a sunflower that measured 26 ft. 4 in. (8.03 m) tall on August 17, 2009.

Did You Know?

The Shortest Sunflower measured just 2.2 in. (56 mm) high. The Largest Sunflower Head had a 32.25 in. (82 cm) diameter.

ACTIVITIES

1. How many more inches of height would make the Tallest Sunflower 30 feet tall?

   _____

2. The word *sunflower* is a compound word made from two smaller words. Use these words to write three compound words: *side, honey, sun, bee, out, shine.*

   _____   _____   _____

Heaviest Apple

Photo: Guinness World Records Limited

Chisato Iwasaki (Japan) presented an apple weighing 4 lb. 1 oz. (1.849 kg) on October 24, 2005.

Did You Know?

Apples are a good source of vitamin C, which helps to heal wounds and keeps bones and teeth healthy.

CHECK THIS OUT!

An average apple weighs about one-third of a pound. This size is a bit small for Chisato Iwasaki (Japan). An apple on his farm grew bigger and bigger, until October 24, 2005, when it won a record for the world's Heaviest Apple. It weighed 4 pounds, 1 ounce! The apple was so big and heavy you would need two hands to hold it!

But that's not the only heavy fruit on record. The world's Heaviest Pear is even bigger than the apple, weighing in at 4 pounds, 8 ounces on May 6, 1999, in New South Wales, Australia. The pear was grown on a 120-year-old tree, which, in 1979, produced a previous record holder at 3 pounds, 1 ounce.

(ACTIVITIES)

1. Which of the following weighs about the same as the world's Heaviest Apple?

   a. a dictionary

   b. a sheet of paper

   c. a car

   d. a box of cereal

2. It takes about two pounds of apples to make a nine-inch apple pie. If Iwasaki had used his apple, how many apple pies could he make? Write an equation to show how you know.

   _____

3. One pound is 16 ounces. How much does the world's Heaviest Apple weigh in ounces?

   _____

4. An average of 65 apples per person are consumed in America each year. How many apples do you eat in a week? Multiply that number by 52 weeks in a year. Do you eat more or fewer apples than the average person?

   _____

5. You may have heard the popular saying, "An apple a day keeps the doctor away." In your own words, what do you think this means?

   _____

   _____

6. Circle your favorite apple treats.

   apple pie

   apple butter

   apple slices with peanut butter

   apple juice

   apple jelly

   cinnamon apples

Longest-Lasting Lightning Storm

Photo: ©2000 Photodisc, Inc.

The longest-lasting lightning storm raged in Saturn's upper atmosphere for more than eight months in 2009. The storm made lightning bolts that were about 10,000 times stronger than those on Earth.

Did You Know?

A bolt of lightning can stretch more than five miles long, and can contain 100 million volts of electricity!

ACTIVITIES

1. Eight months is what fraction of a year?

   _____

2. What planet is sixth from the sun in our solar system?

   _____

3. What two planets are closest to Earth?

   _____   _____

Heaviest Cabbage

Photo: Guinness World Records Limited

Steven Hubacak (USA) presented a cabbage head at the Alaska State Fair weighing 127 lb. (57.61 kg) on September 4, 2009.

Did You Know?

The first Cabbage Patch Kids were called *Little People*. They were first sold at arts and crafts fairs by the college student who made them by hand.

ACTIVITIES

1. How many more pounds would need to be added for the cabbage to weigh 150 pounds?

   _____

2. Cabbage is eaten around the world. Circle a cabbage dish you would like to try.

   kimchi (Korea)   **sauerkraut** (Germany)

   corned beef and cabbage (Ireland)   **egg roll** (China)

   coleslaw (United States)   **borscht** (Russia)

Highest Tsunami Wash

Photo: Image used under license from Shutterstock.com

A giant landslide caused a tsunami (giant wave) along the Lituya Bay, Alaska, on July 9, 1958. It was 1,719 ft. (524 m) high and moved at 100 mph (161 km/h).

Did You Know?

The waves of a tsunami can roll in the open sea as fast as 450 mph (724 km/h), and can be as high as 100 ft. (30.5 m) when they hit shore.

ACTIVITIES

1. Tsunamis can happen in coastal areas. Circle a weather event that has happened close to your home.

   earthquake   **volcano**

   tornado   **flood**

   hurricane   **drought**

2. The tsunami moved at 100 miles per hour. About how fast does a car usually travel on the highway?

Most Expensive Fungus Species

Photo: Guinness World Records Limited

The white truffle is an edible fungus that costs up to $3,000 per kilogram. They are only found in certain regions of Italy. They can only be found with the help of trained dogs because they grow about a foot underground.

Did You Know?

A hot dog sold for $69 at a New York City restaurant. The foot-long hot dog was served on a pretzel roll grilled in white truffle butter.

ACTIVITIES

1. Look at a menu for your favorite restaurant. You may be able to find one online. What is the most expensive item on the menu?

   _____

2. White truffles grow underground. What else do you find deep underground? Draw an underground scene.

Largest Dome Igloo

Photo: Guinness World Records Limited

"The Gloo Crew" of Bellevue, Wisconsin, constructed the igloo in 70 days. The inside of the igloo had a diameter of 27 ft. 2 in. (8.3 m) and a height of 17 ft. 4 in. (5.3 m) when it was measured on February 22, 2010.

Did You Know?

Igloo is the Inuit word for "house." Most Inuit people live today in wood, stone, or cement buildings, not snow igloos.

CHECK THIS OUT!

Do you live where there is ice in the winter? For some people, ice has an important purpose. It is used to build igloos, or dome-shaped houses. The Largest Dome Igloo ever recorded was built in Canada. It was almost wide enough to fit two cars end to end!

This igloo was built during a competition between different teams. The winning team had 70 volunteers. They spent 50 hours and used 2,000 blocks of ice.

The hard-working team did a lot of planning. Their finished igloo was safe and solid. It could hold more than 200 people at a time. It stood for 59 days before the warm April weather caused it to collapse.

ACTIVITIES

1. The finished igloo could hold more than 2,000 people at once. True or false? Circle your answer.

true   false

2. In the passage on page 46, the word *collapse* means:

   a. fall down

   b. freeze

   c. full of holes

   d. inflate

3. Why is Canada a better place to build igloos than Mexico?

   _____

4. Circle five words you read on page 46 to complete the word search. Use the word bank to help you.

igloo   Inuit   house   snow   Wisconsin

```
I  H  O  U  S  E  W  P  O
G  T  K  C  N  M  K  R  E
L  V  D  G  O  O  I  R  W
O  B  F  A  W  S  X  E  B
O  J  K  I  N  U  I  T  G
W  I  S  C  O  N  S  I  N
O  N  W  S  N  O  M  P  T
```

5. Imagine you are the leader of a team that is trying to build the biggest igloo ever. Write a list of rules for your team to follow.

   _____

   _____

Most Electricity Generated by Pedaling on Bicycles for 24 Hours

Photo: Guinness World Records Limited

Ender Werbung GmbH staff and visitors (Austria) generated 12,953 watt hours of electricity by pedaling on 21 bicycles in 24 hours on April 4, 2008, at the Dornbirner Messe Fair, Dornbirn, Austria.

Did You Know?

It is estimated that, in a year, a bicycle spinning class of 20 people could light 72 homes for a month.

ACTIVITIES

1. A 100-watt light bulb uses 100 watts of electricity each hour. About how many 100-watt light bulbs could be lit for one hour with the electricity generated from the bicycles? Use a calculator to find out. Round to the nearest whole number.

   _____

2. The cyclists pedaled for 24 hours. How many days is that?

   _____

Heaviest Sweet Potato

Photo: Guinness World Records Limited

On March 8, 2004, Manuel Pérez Pérez (Spain) presented a sweet potato that weighed 81 lb. 9 oz. (37 kg).

Did You Know?
Sweet potatoes are not potatoes! They are part of the morning glory family, a flowering vine.

ACTIVITIES

1. How many more ounces would make the Heaviest Sweet Potato weigh 82 pounds?

   _____

2. How many groups of 9 are in 81?

   _____

3. Sweet potatoes are often eaten at Thanksgiving. What is your favorite Thanksgiving food?

   _____

Largest Land Vehicle

Photo: Guinness World Records Limited

The RB293 bucket wheel excavator weighs 31.3 million lb. (14,196 metric tons), is 722 ft. (220 m) long, and 310 ft. (94.5 m) tall. The bucket wheel alone measures 71 ft. (21.6 m) across!

Did You Know?

This huge machine is mighty but slow—it moves less than 1 mi. (1.6 km) per hour. You can walk faster than that!

ACTIVITIES

1. The excavator weighs over 31 million pounds. To write one million, fill in each blank with a O.

    1,_____ _____ _____, _____ _____ _____

2. What does *excavate* mean? Research to find out.

    _____

3. What do you think the RB293 could help build?

    _____

Tallest Zinnia

Photo: Guinness World Records Limited

On October 23, 2008, the tallest zinnia measured 12 ft. 8 in. (3.86 m) tall in Riegelwood, North Carolina. The record is held by Everett W. Wallace, Jr. and Melody Wagner (both USA).

Did You Know?
Another name for the zinnia is "old maid flower."

ACTIVITIES

1. *Zinnia* begins with z. Write other words you know that begin with z.

   _____   _____   _____

   _____   _____   _____

2. Give the height of the Tallest Zinnia in inches.

   _____

3. Is the ceiling at your home taller or shorter that 12 feet? Circle your answer.

   taller   **shorter**

Largest Living Tree

GENERAL SHERMAN

Photo: Image used under license from Shutterstock.com

General Sherman, a giant sequoia, grows in Sequoia National Park in California. It stands 271 ft. (82.6 m) tall, has a diameter of 27 ft. 2 in. (8.2 m), and has a circumference of approximately 85 ft. (25.9 m). The tree is thought to be 2,100 years old.

Did You Know?

If you were able to fill the trunk of General Sherman with water, it would be enough water to fill 8,844 bathtubs!

CHECK THIS OUT!

Redwood trees are the largest trees in the world. They are taller than the Statue of Liberty. The two kinds of redwoods are coastal redwoods and giant sequoias. The giant sequoia is named for a famous Native American named *Sequoyah*. He was a member of the Cherokee nation. In 1821, he created an alphabet. The alphabet helped the Cherokee people read, write, and record their history.

The largest living sequoia is named *General Sherman*. It has a diameter that is wider than a two-lane road! Its full weight, with the roots, is about four million pounds. That is almost as much as 1,000 family cars!

1. The largest trees in the world are the

    a. redwood trees.

    b. red oak trees.

    c. birch trees.

    d. cherry trees.

2. The giant sequoia General Sherman is found in California. True or false? Circle your answer.

    true   **false**

3. Design a birdhouse that you think would be suitable to hang on General Sherman. Draw it here.

4. General Sherman is 271 feet tall. How tall are you? In inches, how much taller is General Sherman?

    _____

5. Imagine standing at the base of General Sherman and looking up toward its uppermost branches. Write a paragraph describing how you would feel.

    _____

    _____

    _____

    _____

Largest Tomato Plant

Photo: Guinness World Records Limited

At the Epcot Science Project at Walt Disney World Resort in Lake Buena Vista, Florida, the largest tomato plant covered an area of 610.63 sq. ft. (56.73 m²) on March 27, 2007.

Did You Know?

By the time the greenhouse's biggest tomato plant was 16 months old, the tree had yielded 32,000 tomatoes!

ACTIVITIES

1. Circle your favorite foods made with tomatoes.

spaghetti with sauce   **pizza**

burger with ketchup   **fresh tomato salad**

meatball sandwich   **tomato soup**

2. Write the names of four vegetables you would like to grow in a garden.

_____   _____

_____   _____

Greatest Snowfall for a Single Snowstorm

Photo: Comstock, Inc.

From February 13 to 19, 1959, a snowstorm at the Mt. Shasta Ski Bowl, California, yielded 189 in. (4.8 m) of snow.

Did You Know?

Pink, brown, and even yellow snow has fallen in southern Russia. Gusts of sand and dust blow in from Africa to create these colors of snow.

ACTIVITIES

1. About how many feet of snow fell during the record storm? Use a calculator to find out. Round to the nearest tenth.

   _____

2. The record snowstorm happened in 1959. How many years ago was that?

   _____

3. Write what you would do to play in the snow.

   _____

Heaviest Squash

On September 21, 2007, Bradley Wursten (Netherlands) presented a squash that weighed 1,234 lb. (559.73 kg).

Photo: Guinness World Records Limited

Did You Know?

Many flowers can be eaten and are sometimes added to stir-fry dishes, pancake batter, or salads. Squash blossoms are sometimes dipped in batter and fried.

ACTIVITIES

1. Does the heaviest squash weigh more or less than one ton? Circle your answer.

   less than one ton   **more than one ton**

2. How many more pounds would make the squash weigh 1,500 pounds?

   _____

3. The word *squash* can be a noun and a verb. Write a definition for each.

   squash (n.): _____

   squash (v.): _____

Largest Tree Transplanted

Photo: Guinness World Records Limited

Old Glory measured 58 ft. (17.67 m) tall, 104 ft. (31.6 m) wide, and weighed approximately 916,000 lb. (415.5 metric tons) when it was transplanted on January 20, 2004. It was between 180 and 220 years old.

Did You Know?

This oak tree was moved because of a road-widening project, at a cost of $1 million!

ACTIVITIES

1. This tree was named *Old Glory*. What other object is commonly called *Old Glory*?

   _____

2. Old Glory is an oak tree. Which one is the oak leaf? Color it.

Largest Snowball

Photo: Guinness World Records Limited

On February 10, 2006, college students in Houghton, Michigan, rolled a snowball with a circumference of 21 ft. 3 in. (6.48 m).

Did You Know?

A woman from Lakeland, Florida, has an odd "pet" in her freezer— a snowball she made in 1977.

CHECK THIS OUT!

The students at Michigan Tech University planned a huge ball. They were not going to dance, though. They wanted to break the record for the world's Largest Snowball. On February 10, 2006, students, teachers, and other citizens met on a field. Altogether, 3,745 people gathered.

First, some people rolled a huge snowball. At 21 feet, 3 inches, it set a new record for the world's Largest Snowball, beating the old record of 16 feet, 9 inches. Next, everyone started throwing snowballs before finally lying on the ground and making snow angels. Everyone was having a ball!

ACTIVITIES

1. Is the circumference of the snowball closer to 21 feet or 22 feet? Circle your answer.

21 feet   **22 feet**

2. How much larger is the new record snowball than the old record snowball? Write an equation to show how you know.

_____

_____

3. Which of the following faces would you see if the world's Largest Snowball were cut top to bottom and separated?

a.

b.

c.

d.

4. A *ball* is a spherical body or shape. What is another definition of *ball*?

_____

5. Three-thousand seven-hundred forty-five people gathered together to set this world record. What was the last thing you did as part of a group? Did you enjoy it? Explain why or why not.

_____

_____

_____

Largest Cucumber Plant

Photo: Guinness World Records Limited

In July 2006, at the Epcot Science Project at Walt Disney World Resort in Lake Buena Vista, Florida, the largest cucumber plant covered an area of 610.31 sq. ft. (56.7 m²).

Did You Know?

The longest cucumber measured 41.25 in. (104.78 cm) long. It was grown in a piece of gutter pipe.

ACTIVITIES

1. What do you get when you slice cucumbers and soak them in a mixture of vinegar, spices, sugar, and salt?

   _____

2. Disney World's Epcot theme park has Future World (which focuses on hi-tech inventions) and World Showcase (which features countries such as Mexico, Norway, Morocco, and China). Which area would you visit first? Explain your answer.

   _____

   _____

Largest Permanent Hedge Maze

Photo: Guinness World Records Limited

The Pineapple Garden Maze at the Dole Plantation in Wahiawa, Hawaii, has a total area of 3.15 acres (12,747.59 m²). The total path length is 2.46 mi. (3.962 km). The maze opened in 1997 and expanded in size in July 2007.

Did You Know?

There are clues at eight secret stations along the way through the Pineapple Garden Maze. People who can find their way through this maze quickly win prizes!

ACTIVITIES

1. The path through the maze is about 2.5 miles long. If you walked at a rate of five miles per hour, how long would it take you?

_____

2. Find a way through this maze.

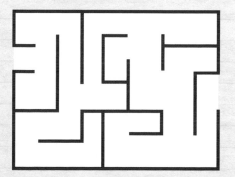

Heaviest Pepper

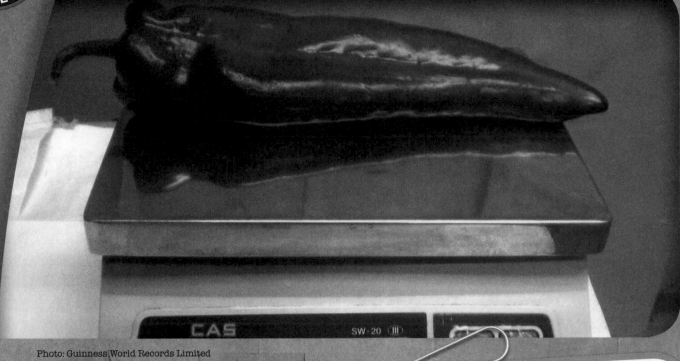

Photo: Guinness World Records Limited

On November 6, 2009, Edward Curry (USA) presented a pepper that weighed 10.2 oz. (289 g).

Did You Know?

The world's hottest chili pepper, a Thai pepper called *bhut jolokia*, is so hot you have to wear gloves to handle it.

ACTIVITIES

1. Write < or > to complete the statement.

Heaviest Pepper one pound

2. Do you like spicy hot foods? Explain why or why not.

_____

_____

3. How many times can you say this tongue twister fast?

Peter Piper picked a peck of pickled peppers.

Longest Board Cut From One Tree

Photo: Guinness World Records Limited

The board was 133 ft. 11 in. (40.815 m).
It was cut from one tree on March 13, 2009,
in Wilkowo, Poland.

Did You Know?

There are three redwood trees
in California that are so big
a car can drive through them!

ACTIVITIES

1. Write what you would build from a very long board.

   _____

2. How many more inches would make the longest board 150 feet?

   _____

3. Do you think people should cut down tall trees for wood? Explain why
   or why not.

   _____

Fastest Growing Plant

Photo: ©2004 Dynamic Graphics, Inc.

One species of bamboo has been found to grow as fast as 36 in. (91 cm) per day. There are over 1,000 species of bamboo on Earth.

Did You Know?

A panda eats a lot of bamboo. To get to the tender meat inside, it holds the stalk with its five fingers and then peels off the tough layers with its teeth.

ACTIVITIES

1. How many feet can the bamboo grow in three days?

_____

2. What is the square root of 36?

_____

3. Giant pandas sleep as much as 12 hours each day. How many hours are they awake each day?

_____

Photo: Guinness World Records Limited

WACKY SOCIETY

Photo: Guinness World Records Limited

Most People on Unicycles

Photo: Guinness World Records Limited

There were 1,142 people riding unicycles simultaneously at an event in Regensburg, Germany, on June 12, 2005.

Did You Know?

Some unicyclists call bicycles "unicycles with a training wheel."

ACTIVITIES

1. What series of three things can you and a friend do simultaneously?

   _____

2. It takes many hours of practice to learn to ride a unicycle. What have you practiced for many hours?

   _____

3. Write two adjectives that describe your bike, scooter, skateboard, or other prized possession.

   _____   _____

Most Participants in a Snowboard Race

Photo: Guinness World Records Limited

A snowboard race with 88 participants was held in Christchurch, New Zealand, on October 6, 2007.

Did You Know?
Snowboarding is one of the fastest growing sports in the U.S. It became a Winter Olympic Sport in 1998.

ACTIVITIES

1. If one snowboarder launched every 30 seconds, how many minutes would it take 88 snowboarders to launch?

_____

2. What country is New Zealand's closest neighbor?

_____

3. Would you rather ride a surfboard, a skateboard, or a snowboard? Explain why.

_____

Most People Carving Pumpkins Simultaneously

Photo: Guinness World Records Limited

On Halloween in 2005, 965 students carved pumpkins at the Malvern Town Centre in Scarborough, Ontario, Canada.

Did You Know?
The first jack-o'-lantern may have been carved from a turnip.

ACTIVITIES

1. If each carver removed 50 seeds from a pumpkin, how many seeds would there be in all?

_____

2. Circle words that describe a jack-o'-lantern you would like to carve.

terrifying	toothy	grinning
surprised	friendly	menacing
goofy	grim	happy

Largest Human Wheelbarrow Race

Photo: Guinness World Records Limited

The largest human wheelbarrow race had 777 pairs. It happened in New South Wales, Australia, on November 6, 2009.

Did You Know?
Some say the wheelbarrow was invented over 2,000 years ago.

ACTIVITIES

1. How many individuals participated in the race?

   _____

2. Australian and North American seasons are opposites. January is winter in the U.S. and summer in Australia. May is spring in the U.S. and

   _____ in Australia.

3. Circle ways you would like to race with a partner.

   three-legged race   **piggy back race**

   wheelbarrow race   **relay race**

Most People on One Motorcycle

Photo: Guinness World Records Limited

The most people on one moving motorcycle is 54 and was achieved by the "Tornadoes" Army Service Corps Motorcycle Display Team (all India) in Bangalore, India, on November 28, 2010.

Did You Know?

The first motorcycle was sold in 1894.

CHECK THIS OUT!

Some people like to take risks by performing stunts on moving vehicles. Evel Knievel (United States) was one of those people. The daredevil performed over 75 ramp-to-ramp motorcycle jumps in his career. Knievel holds the world record for Most Broken Bones in a Lifetime! He suffered 433 bone fractures by age 37.

The members of the "Tornadoes" Army Service Corps Motorcycle Display Team in India are also in the record books for their feats on a motorcycle. The 54 men all rode a single motorcycle a distance of 0.68 miles (1,100 m). The motorcycle was modified with a platform around the edge to carry all the people. No one touched the ground during the attempt, so no one was disqualified.

ACTIVITIES

1. What is a *daredevil*? What are some pros and cons of being a daredevil?

_____

_____

2. The people who set the record for the most people on one moving motorcycle are from _____ .

   a. India

   b. USA

   c. China

   d. Japan

3. Circle five words you read on page 70 to complete the word search. Use the word bank to help you.

   Evel motorcycle India fractures jumps

L	O	P	T	E	V	E	L	K	Q
M	O	T	O	R	C	Y	C	L	E
E	P	I	M	N	C	X	W	A	S
K	O	N	J	U	M	P	S	U	D
H	A	D	O	K	J	H	N	B	V
E	W	I	O	L	U	C	E	A	S
F	R	A	C	T	U	R	E	S	L
R	D	E	S	C	Z	G	T	Y	I

4. The "Tornadoes" Army Service Corps Motorcycle Display Team rode a single motorcycle 0.68 miles. How long does it take you to run that far? Ask an adult to time you.

_____

Most People Doing Cartwheels (Mass Participation)

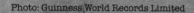

Photo: Guinness World Records Limited

At an event in Schothorst, Netherlands, on July 10, 2009, 482 people performed cartwheels simultaneously.

Did You Know?

When you do a cartwheel, you briefly pass through a handstand position.

ACTIVITIES

1. How many cartwheels, handstands, or somersaults can you and a friend perform in three minutes?

   _____

2. To write directions, your words must be precise and logical. Write step-by-step directions for doing a cartwheel, handstand, or somersault.

   _____

   _____

   _____

Longest Chain of People Licking Lollipops

Photo: Guinness World Records Limited

A chain of 12,831 people licked lollipops on September 7, 2008, in Valladolid, Spain.

Did You Know?
National Lollipop Day is celebrated in the U.S. on July 20th.

ACTIVITIES

1. If 30 people could stand in each row, how many rows would be needed for all the lollipop-lickers? Round to the nearest whole number.

   _____

2. If 5,000 people chose a cherry lollipop, how many chose some other flavor?

   _____

3. What is your favorite lollipop flavor?

   _____

Most People Folding T-Shirts

Photo: Guinness World Records Limited

On May 14, 2009, at a shopping center in London, United Kingdom, 275 people folded T-shirts at the same time.

Did You Know?

T-shirts were once worn only as underwear. James Dean shocked people by wearing one in the 1955 movie *Rebel Without a Cause*.

ACTIVITIES

1. If one person took 9.5 seconds to fold a shirt, one took 11 seconds, one took 12 seconds, and one took 14.5 seconds, what was the average time it took to fold a shirt?

   _____

2. If each member of your family wears one shirt each day, how many shirts are worn in two weeks?

   _____

3. Write what you do to help with the laundry.

   _____

Most People Dribbling Basketballs at the Same Time

Photo: Guinness World Records Limited

At an event organized by the United Nations, 7,556 people dribbled basketballs in Rafah, Gaza Strip, Palestine.

Did You Know?

The United Nations was founded in 1945 after World War II by 51 countries committed to international peace and security.

ACTIVITIES

1. If each person dribbled a basketball 12 times at the event, how many dribbles were done in all?

   _____

2. Write < or > to complete the statement.

   7,556 $\frac{3}{4}$ of 10,000

3. How many times can you dribble a ball without missing?

   _____

Most People Buried in Sand Simultaneously

Photo: Guinness World Records Limited

The most people buried in the sand simultaneously is 517. The event took place at the Clogherhead Prawn Festival 2010 in Louth, Ireland, on July 17, 2010.

Did You Know?

The sand on the coast of Namibia (in southwest Africa) contains diamonds.

CHECK THIS OUT!

Have you ever been to the beach? Many families enjoy visiting the beach for vacations during the summer months. It can be fun to splash in the ocean, relax on the sand, or even go surfing. Some children also enjoy building sandcastles or burying each other in the sand. This is when your whole body is covered in sand except for your head!

People at the Clogherhead Prawn Festival also enjoy being buried in the sand. More than 500 people were buried in the sand on July 17, 2010. Originally, only 480 participants were expected. However, 37 people who arrived that day also wanted to join in on the world record attempt, so they were added as well.

ACTIVITIES

1. How many people were buried in the sand for this world record?

   a. 480

   b. 517

   c. 500

   d. 37

2. Unscramble words you read on page 76.

   hacbe _____

   ivestfla _____

   dasn _____

   ataocvnis _____

   dansssstelca _____

3. Have you been to the beach? If so, what did you like about it? If you have not visited the beach, would you like to? Explain why or why not.

   _____

   _____

   _____

4. Circle things you could do at the beach.

   swim

   ski

   surf

   build sandcastles

   relax

   make snow angels

Most People Twirling Batons

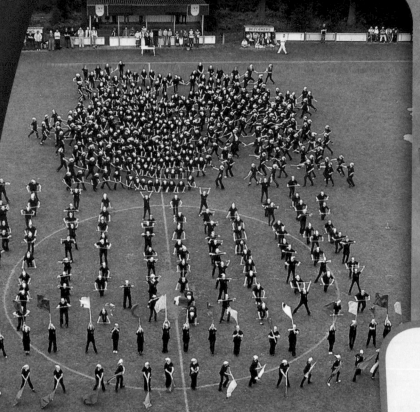

Photo: Guinness World Records Limited

On May 16, 2004, 1,012 people twirled batons in Bakel, Netherlands.

Did You Know?
People from the Netherlands are called *the Dutch*.

ACTIVITIES

1. How many more baton twirlers would be needed to make the total number 1,500?

   _____

2. What is the largest city in the Netherlands? Look at a map for help.

   _____

3. What could you do to participate in a parade?

   _____

Most Custard Pies Thrown by Two Teams of 10

Photo: Guinness World Records Limited

The largest custard pie fight involved 3,320 pies thrown by two teams of 10 in three minutes in Bolton, United Kingdom, in 2005.

Did You Know?

A famous pie fight can be seen in the 1941 Three Stooges comedy film *In the Sweet Pie and Pie.*

ACTIVITIES

1. Twenty people threw 3,320 pies. How many pies did each person throw?

   _____

2. The pie fight lasted for three minutes. About how many pies were thrown each minute? Round to the nearest whole number.

   _____

3. Would you rather throw a pie or get "pied"? Explain why.

   _____

Longest Human Chain (Length)

Photo: Guinness World Records Limited

In 2004, over five million people joined hands to form a chain 652.4 mi. (1,050 km) long from Teknaf to Tentulia, Bangladesh.

Did You Know?

About a third of the land in Bangladesh floods each year during the monsoon rainy season.

ACTIVITIES

1. Hold hands with a friend, stretching your arms wide. Have another friend measure you. What is the total span of your arms in inches?

   _____

2. Using your answer to #1, estimate about how many people would be needed to form a human chain along a city block that is $\frac{1}{8}$ of a mile (660 feet) long.

   _____

Largest Game of Simon Says

Photo: Guinness World Records Limited

At the Utah Summer Games Opening Ceremony in 2007, 12,215 people played Simon Says.

Did You Know?
The game Simon Says may have its origins in the Hebrew name *Shim'on*, which means "listening."

ACTIVITIES

1. Write about a time you heard something incorrectly. Did your mistake cause any problems?

   _____

   _____

2. If $\frac{1}{5}$ of the Simon Says players made an error for each command, how many people made an error for any one command?

   _____

Largest Pizza Delivery

Photo: Guinness World Records Limited

The largest pizza delivery was made by Papa John's. The company delivered 13,500 pizzas to the NASSCO Shipyard in San Diego, California, on June 8, 2006.

Did You Know?
Some gourmet pizzas are topped with oysters, crayfish, dandelions, sprouts, eggplant, artichoke hearts, and tuna.

CHECK THIS OUT!

Pepperoni, sausage, bacon, onions, mushrooms, anchovies, pineapples, green peppers...do you have an idea of what this passage could be about? Of course! It's pizza!

Pizza is a popular food in the United States—93 percent of Americans have eaten pizza in the last month, and many of those pizzas are delivered. Each year, the most popular days to order pizza delivery are Super Bowl Sunday, New Year's Eve, Halloween, the night before Thanksgiving, and New Year's Day.

About three billion pizzas are sold annually in the United States, and in 2006, 13,500 of those pizzas were delivered to some hungry ship builders. The pizzas were ordered in celebration of the completion of the *USNS Lewis and Clark* auxiliary ship.

ACTIVITIES

1. Pepperoni is said to be the most popular pizza topping. What is your favorite topping? Explain why.

_____

2. If 93% of your class at school has eaten pizza in the last month, about how many students have not eaten pizza in that time frame?

_____

3. Unscramble words you read on page 82.

cnoba   _____

ionosn   _____

vehncasoi   _____

smsohuorm   _____

eagusas   _____

prpeonipe   _____

ngere rspppee   _____

4. Why do you think Super Bowl Sunday is a popular day to order pizza?

_____

_____

5. If three billion pizzas are sold each year, about how many are sold per day? Round to the nearest whole number.

_____

Largest Gathering of People Dressed as Gorillas

Photo: Guinness World Records Limited

The Mountain Gorilla Conservation Fund organized an event in Denver, Colorado, in 2009 at which 1,061 people dressed as gorillas.

Did You Know?

The record-setting event was named *The Denver Gorilla Run.*

ACTIVITIES

1. People have written many stories, songs, and movies about gorillas, including *The Planet of the Apes* films. What is your favorite story or movie that features a gorilla?

   _____

2. Gorillas are large mammals that live in the forests of Africa. Write the names of four more African mammals.

   _____   _____

   _____   _____

Largest Simultaneous Yo-Yo

Photo: Guinness World Records Limited

At the 2010 National Scout Jamboree in Fort A.P. Hill, Virginia, 2,036 Boy Scouts yo-yoed at the same time.

Did You Know?

An ancient Greek vase from 440 BC shows a boy playing with a yo-yo.

ACTIVITIES

1. If each yo-yo had 18 inches of string, how many feet of string would be needed for all 2,036 yo-yos?

   _____

2. The word *yo-yo* has repeating syllables. Other words like it are *putt-putt*, *mama*, and *bonbon*. Write four more words with repeating syllables.

   _____   _____

   _____   _____

Largest "YMCA" Dance

Photo: Guinness World Records Limited

At an event organized by the Sun Bowl Association in Texas, 40,148 people did the "YMCA" dance on December 31, 2008.

Did You Know?

YMCA stands for "Young Men's Christian Association." It was founded in 1844 by George Williams in London, England.

ACTIVITIES

1. What letters other than Y-M-C-A can you form with your body? Use your body to spell words for a friend to guess. Take turns. What was the most difficult word to guess?

   _____

2. The record was set in a stadium. If the stadium had 16 sections, about how many people could sit in each section? Use a calculator to find out. Round to the nearest whole number.

   _____

Largest Gathering of People Dressed as Superman

Photo: Guinness World Records Limited

Two hundred eighty-eight people dressed as Superman at an event in Omeath, County Louth, Ireland, on August 21, 2010.

Did You Know?

Superman is called *The Man of Steel*. His powers are flight, super speed, heat vision, x-ray vision, and invulnerability.

ACTIVITIES

1. What would you do right now if you had Superman's powers?

   _____

2. Who is your favorite superhero? What are his or her powers? Does he or she have a nickname?

   _____

3. If $\frac{1}{6}$ of the Supermen were age 12 and younger, how many of the Supermen would be in the under-12 category?

   _____

87

Most Participants in a Multi-Legged Race

Photo: Guinness World Records Limited

The most participants in a multi-legged race was achieved by 305 people in Yoyogi, Shibuya, Japan, on November 28, 2010.

Did You Know?
Japan is made up of over 6,000 islands.

CHECK THIS OUT!

You may think a three-legged race looks easy—until you try it! In a three-legged race, two partners are tied together. The left ankle of one runner is bound to the right ankle of his or her partner in order to form "three" legs. To win the race, the runners must work together to move in unison without falling over. Teamwork is key!

Now, imagine a multi-legged race. In a multi-legged race, you aren't just partnered up with one other person; you're partnered with more than one! That means both of your ankles may be tied to someone else. On November 28, 2010, 305 participants ran a multi-legged race all at the same time! The participants were invited online, through social networking sites, brochures, and word-of-mouth.

1. Name four ways participants were invited to the multi-legged race.

_____   _____

_____   _____

2. If 305 people were involved in a race, how many legs were there in all?

_____

3. What does _unison_ mean? Write your own sentence using that word.

_____

_____

4. Circle five words you read on page 88 to complete the word search. Use the word bank to help you.

race   ankles   teamwork   runners   partner

```
P  A  R  T  N  E  R  L  D
T  N  T  G  W  S  C  V  M
U  K  U  O  M  N  W  E  L
M  L  R  U  N  N  E  R  S
T  E  A  M  W  O  R  K  O
L  S  C  R  M  U  Y  B  V
L  P  E  Y  U  F  S  A  W
```

5. Try it out! Partner up with a friend and have a three-legged race. Is it easy or hard to do? Does it get easier with practice?

_____

Largest Easter Egg Hunt

Photo: Guinness World Records Limited

In 2007, 9,753 children searched for 501,000 eggs at Cypress Gardens Adventure Park in Winter Haven, Florida.

Did You Know?

Each year, 90 million chocolate bunnies and 16 billion jelly beans are made for Easter. Most people like red jelly beans best.

ACTIVITIES

1. Put small objects inside plastic eggs or other little containers. Have a friend shake and guess what's inside. What was hardest to guess?

_____

2. About how many eggs were hidden for each child at the Largest Easter Egg Hunt? Use a calculator to find out. Round to the nearest whole number.

_____

Largest Gathering of Pirates

Photo: Guinness World Records Limited

In the beach town of Hastings in East Sussex, United Kingdom, 6,166 people gathered to dress like pirates on August 6, 2010.

Did You Know?

Many pirate ships were democracies. Everyone voted about where to sail, who would be captain, and how treasure would be divided.

ACTIVITIES

1. During the golden age of piracy, pirates plundered around the islands of Cuba, Jamaica, and Haiti. What other countries start with *C*, *J*, or *H*?

   _____

2. It's fun to talk like a pirate! Use the dictionary below to write a pirate message.

   _____

ahoy: hello

arr: I'm angry

avast: stop and look

aye: yes

land lubber: person who lives on land

smartly: quickly

Largest Tea Party

Photo: Guinness World Records Limited

At Nehru Stadium in Indore, India, 32,681 people participated in a tea party on February 24, 2008.

Did You Know?
After water, tea is the second most popular drink in the world. Over half the world's population drinks a cup of tea each day.

ACTIVITIES

1. Tea bushes grow well in India's hot, dry climate. Find India on a map. What is the capital of that country?

   _____

2. Circle something in each category to describe a tea drink you would like to try.

Temperature:	Tea:	With:
hot	green tea	sugar and cream
iced	black tea	lemon
	oolong tea	mint leaves

Largest Dog Walk (Single Breed)

Photo: Guinness World Records Limited

Seven hundred Labrador retrievers were walked at a charity event in Warsaw, Poland, on August 29, 2010.

Did You Know?

Labrador retrievers love to fetch (*retrieve* is right in their name). They also love to swim. A Lab has webbed feet and a tail like an otter's.

ACTIVITIES

1. If half of the people at the event walked two dogs, and half walked just one dog, how many people participated?

_____

2. Labrador retrievers may have been first bred in the far northeast province of Newfoundland and Labrador, Canada. What province of Canada is closest to your home?

_____

Largest Gathering of People Dressed as Fruits

Photo: Guinness World Records Limited

The largest gathering of people dressed as fruits was achieved by 206 participants in Greenwich, London, United Kingdom, on September 27, 2009.

Did You Know?
Bananas, apples, and watermelons float in water.

CHECK THIS OUT!

If you were in London on September 27, 2009, you might have thought you were going bananas! All 206 participants in the Largest Gathering of People Dressed as Fruits were dressed as—you guessed it!—bananas. The event was organized by Leukemia Research (United Kingdom).

Bananas are a popular fruit. The average American eats 27 pounds of bananas each year! And that's a good thing, because bananas are a good source of vitamin B6, which your brain needs to function properly and make you wise.

There are over 400 banana varieties grown in the world. If all the bananas in the world were placed end-to-end, the banana chain would circle Earth 1,400 times.

(ACTIVITIES)

1. How many bananas does the average American eat per year?

   a. 2 pounds

   b. 7 pounds

   c. 27 pounds

   d. 72 pounds

2. How many banana varieties are grown in the world? Circle your answer.

   more than 300   **more than 1,300**

3. Finish the sentence.

   Bananas are a good source of vitamin _____ .

4. Conduct an experiment! Take two unripe bananas. Put one in the refrigerator and leave one on the counter. Observe the bananas for one week. What happens to both bananas?

   _____

   _____

5. What is your favorite fruit? With an adult, make a smoothie using a banana, your favorite fruit, and some milk or yogurt. List the ingredients you used.

   _____   _____

   _____   _____

   _____   _____

6. Find a map of the world. Where is London? What direction is London from where you live?

   _____

Largest Single - Location Food Drive in 24 Hours

Students at the North Carolina School of Science and Mathematics collected 559,885 lb. (254,493 kg) of food on March 5, 2011.

Did You Know?
The best items to give to a food bank are canned tuna, peanut butter, soup, rice or pasta, cereal, and canned vegetables.

Photo: Guinness World Records Limited

ACTIVITIES

1. Describe a project everyone at your school worked together to complete.

_____

_____

2. Write about a time you volunteered to help others.

_____

_____

_____

Longest Marathon Playing Dodgeball

Photo: Guinness World Records Limited

Two teams in Albany, New York, played dodgeball for 31 hours 11 minutes 13 seconds on April 5–6, 2010.

Did You Know?

Dodgeball is popular in Japan, where elementary school students compete each year for the Kuroneko Cup.

ACTIVITIES

1. Write < or > to complete the statement.

   dodgeball marathon 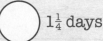 $1\frac{1}{4}$ days

2. If 12 players need 4 balls, how many balls are needed by 144 players?

   _____

3. What is your favorite game to play in the gym or on the playground?

   _____

Most People Brushing Their Teeth

Photo: Guinness World Records Limited

On November 5, 2005, 13,380 people brushed their teeth at the Cuscatlán Stadium in the city of San Salvador in El Salvador.

Did You Know?

Sharks lose teeth throughout their lives. Whenever they lose a tooth, a new one grows to take its place.

ACTIVITIES

1. If each brusher at the stadium spit three times, what was the total number of spits?

   _____

2. If a tube of toothpaste lasts for 36 brushes and you brush twice a day, in how many days will you need a new tube?

   _____

3. List four things you do to keep your teeth healthy.

   _____   _____

   _____   _____

Largest Gathering of Elvis Impersonators

Photo: Guinness World Records Limited

Six hundred forty-five people impersonated Elvis Presley in Las Vegas, Nevada, on November 23, 2010.

Did You Know?

Elvis, "The King of Rock and Roll," recorded music that combined rhythm and blues, pop, country, and gospel.

ACTIVITIES

1. If each person at the event had a costume with 120 sparkly rhinestones, how many rhinestones would there be in all?

   _____

2. Play a game with a friend. Pretend to be a famous person or character. Take turns guessing each other's impersonations. Who was hardest to guess?

   _____

3. What is your favorite song?

Most People Apple Bobbing

Photo: Guinness World Records Limited

The most people apple bobbing is 266 and was achieved by At Work/Talent Recruitment, New Heart for Heywood, and the people of Heywood (all UK), in Heywood, Lancashire, United Kingdom, on September 25, 2010.

Did You Know?

Apples are grown in all 50 U.S. states.

CHECK THIS OUT!

Have you ever bobbed for apples? Apple bobbing is a game usually played around Halloween. It is played by filling a tub or a large bucket with water, and then putting apples in the water. Rather than sinking, the apples will float at the surface. The object of the game is to catch as many apples as you can, but there is one catch—using your hands is not allowed! Players must use their teeth when bobbing for apples.

In September 2010, 266 people set the record for the Most People Apple Bobbing at the same time. Of those 266 people, one participant succeeded in bobbing 10 apples in one minute, seven seconds. That's a pretty amazing feat for using only your teeth!

1. Apples are grown in all 50 states. How many states can you identify in 60 seconds? Ask an adult to time you. Color the states that you can identify correctly.

2. What is the first thing you think of when you hear the word *apple*?

_____

3. Draw a picture to illustrate the expression, "You are the apple of my eye."

Largest Tug-of-War Tournament

Photo: Guinness World Records Limited

A tug-of-war tournament with 1,290 students from two schools in the Netherlands (Het Nieuwe Lyceum and De Werkplaats) was held on November 17, 2010.

Did You Know?
Tug-of-war was part of the Olympic Games from 1900–1920.

ACTIVITIES

1. If an equal number of students from each school competed, how many were from each school?

_____

2. If all the students were divided into 10 teams, how many would be on each team?

_____

3. The Netherlands is on what continent?

_____

Most People Crammed in a Smart Car

Photo: Guinness World Records Limited

Nineteen people crammed into a Smart® car at Defence Authority Creek Club in Karachi, Pakistan, on December 15, 2010.

Did You Know?

In a 1950s fad, college students competed to see how many people could be crammed into a phone booth.

ACTIVITIES

1. If 19 people fit into one Smart car, how many people will fit into eight Smart cars?

_____

2. How many stuffed animals, books, or other objects do you think you can cram into a backpack or suitcase?

_____

3. Test your estimate. How many things fit?

_____

Most People Keeping a Soccer Ball in the Air

Photo: Guinness World Records Limited

In Yanji City, China, 1,062 students and fans at Yanbian University kept soccer balls in the air on July 10, 2010.

Did You Know?

The participants controlled the soccer balls in the air for 11 seconds.

ACTIVITIES

1. If the participants stood in 18 rows, how many people would be in each row?

   _____

2. For how many seconds can you keep a ball or a balloon in the air?

   _____

3. What type of ball do you control best?

   _____

Largest Gathering of People Dressed as Waldo

Photo: Guinness World Records Limited

On April 2, 2009, 1,052 people dressed as Waldo at Rutgers University in New Brunswick, New Jersey.

Did You Know?

British illustrator Martin Handford created the first *Where's Wally?* book in 1987. In North America, the books are called *Where's Waldo?*

ACTIVITIES

1. The word *ironic* can mean "showing an inconsistency between an actual and an expected result." Explain why it is ironic for more than 1,000 people to dress as Waldo.

   _____

   _____

2. Hide an action figure or other toy in plain sight and challenge a friend to find it. Take turns hiding the figure in different areas. In what scene was the figure hardest to spot?

   _____

Most People Blowing a Chewing Gum Bubble Simultaneously

Photo: Guinness World Records Limited

The most people blowing a chewing gum bubble simultaneously is 304 participants and was achieved by Kirkwood Community College (USA) in Cedar Rapids, Iowa, on October 27, 2010.

Did You Know?

Nearly 300 sticks of gum are chewed by the average American each year.

CHECK THIS OUT!

If you were in Iowa on October 27, 2010, you may have heard a *pop* as Kirkwood Community College (United States) burst into the record books.

Over 300 people set a record for Most People Blowing a Chewing Gum Bubble Simultaneously. The event was held at the school's gymnasium during halftime at a volleyball game. Students, volleyball players, and teachers all participated.

However, none of the 304 people were able to blow the largest bubblegum bubble. That record belongs to Chad Fell (United States), who blew a bubble with a diameter of 20 inches without using his hands in Winston County, Alabama, on April 24, 2004. In comparison, the diameter of a dinner plate is about 10 inches. The world's Largest Bubblegum Bubble was twice as big!

ACTIVITIES

Complete the crossword puzzle with words you read on page 106.

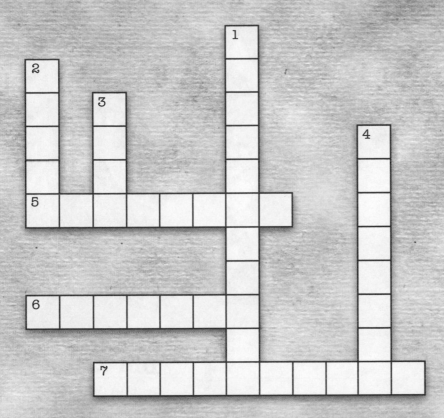

Across

5. Students, volleyball players, and _____ participated in the record attempt.

6. Chad Fell is from this state.

7. People blew a bubble during halftime of a game for this sport.

Down

1. The world's Largest Bubblegum Bubble is twice as big as this.

2. Another word for *pop* is _____.

3. State where Kirkwood Community College is located

4. _____ set the record for the Largest Bubblegum Bubble.

Most People Arm Wrestling

Photo: Guinness World Records Limited

At VIT University in Vellore, Tamilnadu, India, 668 people arm-wrestled on January 27, 2011.

Did You Know?

In the cartoon *Dexter's Laboratory*, Dexter invents a mechanical arm for his dad to use when he arm-wrestles a stronger opponent.

ACTIVITIES

1. How many pairs of people arm-wrestled at the event?

   _____

2. Do you think arm wrestling is a good way to settle a disagreement? Explain why or why not.

   _____

3. Look for India on a map. What long river can be found in northeastern India?

   _____

Most People Blowing Whistles Simultaneously

Photo: Guinness World Records Limited

At Suncorp Stadium in Brisbane, Australia, 37,552 people blew whistles simultaneously on September 5, 2008.

Did You Know?

Whistling can be a sign of happiness. The song "Whistle While You Work" was written for the 1937 Disney film *Snow White and the Seven Dwarfs*.

ACTIVITIES

1. Some people blow whistles as part of their jobs or daily activities. Write four types of people who blow whistles.

   _____   _____

   _____   _____

2. A *whistle blower* is someone who points out bad behavior or injustice. Is it a good idea to be a whistle blower when a classmate at school is mistreated? Explain why or why not.

   _____

Most People Wearing Wigs (Single Venue)

Photo: Guinness World Records Limited

At a National Hockey League game in Philadelphia, Pennsylvania, 9,315 people wore wigs on October 30, 2006.

Did You Know?

In ancient Egypt, men and women wore wigs of human hair, wool, or fibers. The more elaborate the wig, the higher the social status.

ACTIVITIES

1. If every third person at the event wore an orange wig, how many orange wigs would there be?

_____

2. Draw a wacky wig on this head.

Most People Dressed as Smurfs

Photo: Guinness World Records Limited

At Swansea University in Swansea, United Kingdom, 2,510 people dressed as Smurfs on June 8, 2009.

Did You Know?

Smurfs were created by Belgian cartoonist Peyo. He invented the word *smurf* when he couldn't remember the word he wanted to say.

ACTIVITIES

1. How many groups of 10 Smurfs were at the event?

   _____

2. In Smurf language, *smurf* can be any part of speech. For example, if you woke up in a good mood, you could say, "I just smurfed up and I'm feeling smurfy." Write a sentence in which *smurf* or another silly word is used as a noun, a verb, and an adjective.

   _____

   _____

Most People Doing Chest Bumps

Photo: Guinness World Records Limited

The most people doing chest bumps is 446 and was achieved by customers and employees at McDonald's (Australia) in Melbourne, Victoria, Australia, on October 27, 2009.

Did You Know?

National High Five Day occurs each year on the third Thursday in April.

CHECK THIS OUT!

Everyone loves a good celebration. High fives, fist bumps, and chest bumps are a few ways to express excitement with a friend or teammate. There are many stories about the origin of the high five, but one theory is that it began in 1977 between two baseball players on the Los Angeles Dodgers. Since then, the fist bump and chest bump have also grown in popularity.

The record for Most People Doing Chest Bumps stands at 446. McDonald's assistant managers took 5 minutes, 55 seconds to perform 223 chest bumps.

McDonald's isn't the only group in the record books for their celebrations. The most people doing fist bumps simultaneously was achieved by 390 participants (all Australia) in Armidale, New South Wales, Australia, on June 2, 2010.

ACTIVITIES

1. The high five may have been born in 1977. How many years ago was that? Circle your answer.

more than 30   **less than 30**

2. How many people set the record for Most People Doing Chest Bumps?

   a. 555

   b. 223

   c. 390

   d. 446

3. Are you part of a team? What is your role on the team?

   _____

   _____

4. Look at a map of Australia. How many states and mainland territories does it have? Fill in the blanks below.

   _____ **states**   _____ **mainland territories**

5. Now, do some research about Australia. What is the capital? What are some common animals found in Australia? Would you want to visit Australia?

   _____

   _____

   _____

   _____

6. What are the meanings of these Australian slang words?

   G'day: _____   **Rug Rat:** _____

   Sheila: _____   **Croc:** _____

   Bloke: _____   **Uni:** _____

Most People Crammed on an Unmodified Bus

Two hundred nine adults were crammed into a standard single-decker bus in Czestochowa, Poland, on September 12, 2009.

Did You Know?
In the 1930s, Italians designed a triple-decker bus to serve the busy route between Rome and Tivoli, Italy.

Photo: Guinness World Records Limited

ACTIVITIES

1. The record is for an *unmodified* bus. What could be modified, or changed, in a bus to allow more people to fit?

_____

2. If each seat on the bus could hold six people, about how many seats would be needed? Round to the nearest whole number.

_____

3. Look at a map. What large country is west of Poland?

_____

Most People Wearing Groucho Marx Glasses

Photo: Guinness World Records Limited

At an outdoor film festival in Chicago, Illinois, 4,436 people wore Groucho Marx glasses on July 21, 2009.

Did You Know?

Groucho Marx was a comic performer from 1919–1972. He was known for his glasses and painted-on moustache and eyebrows.

ACTIVITIES

1. Groucho Marx said many funny things. He said, "Outside of a dog, a book is man's best friend. Inside of a dog, it's too dark to read." What is your favorite funny saying or joke?

_____

_____

2. How many individual bushy eyebrows were worn by people at the event?

_____

Most People Spinning Tops Simultaneously

Photo: Guinness World Records Limited

At the Tuen Mun Town Plaza in Hong Kong, China, 377 people spun tops at the same time on October 1, 2010.

Did You Know?
A *gyroscope* is a hi-tech top with a motor. Gyroscopes are used in aviation guidance systems and in the Segway® vehicle.

ACTIVITIES

1. If each person at the event spun a top three times, how many spins were completed in all?

   _____

2. Playing with a top lets you explore how things move in our universe. Potential energy changes to kinetic energy when you spin a top. Momentum keeps the top spinning perfectly for a while. What happens as energy begins to lessen?

   _____

Most People Simultaneously Walking on Stilts

Photo: Guinness World Records Limited

Cirque du Soleil organized 737 people walking on stilts in Montreal, Quebec, Canada, on June 16, 2009.

Did You Know?

French shepherds used to wear stilts to help them see further into the distance while watching herds of sheep.

ACTIVITIES

1. If stilts added $2\frac{1}{2}$ feet to your height, how tall would you be?

   _____

2. Have an adult help you make low stilts. Use a hammer and nail to punch a hole on each side of two cans or sturdy plastic containers. For each stilt, thread a long string through the holes. Step on the stilts, holding the strings in your hands. Was it easy or difficult to walk on your stilts?

   _____

Most People Scuba Diving Simultaneously

Photo: Guinness World Records Limited

The most people scuba diving simultaneously is 2,486 and was achieved in Malalayang Beach, Manado, Indonesia, on August 17, 2009.

Did You Know?

Scuba is an acronym that stands for "Self-Contained Underwater Breathing Apparatus."

CHECK THIS OUT!

Indonesia is often referred to as the world's largest archipelago, or chain of islands. It consists of more than 17,000 islands! Indonesia is known for the beauty and diversity of its marine life. When you're scuba diving in Manado, you can see over 70 percent of all fish species that exist in that part of the Pacific Ocean!

The event that set the record for the Most People Scuba Diving Simultaneously also included a full ceremony performed underwater by the 2,486 divers. The event was organized in celebration of the Indonesian Independence Day. Once the scuba divers reached the bottom of the sea, at a depth of about 50 feet, they saluted the red and white Indonesian flag underwater.

ACTIVITIES

1. What does *scuba* stand for?

   a. Self-Contained Underwater Breathing Apparatus

   b. Self-Contained Underwater Breathing Device

   c. Super Cool Underwater Breathing Adventure

   d. Self-Contained Undersea Breathing Apparatus

2. Finish the sentence.

   Indonesia is often referred to as the world's largest _____ .

3. Draw a picture of what you might see while scuba diving.

4. Look up a picture of the Indonesian flag. Draw it here.

Most People Balancing Books on Their Heads

Photo: Guinness World Records Limited

Nine hundred thirty-nine people balanced books on their heads in Silver City, Philippines, on June 28, 2008.

Did You Know?
To maintain your sense of balance, your brain uses information it takes in from your eyes, muscles, and nervous system.

ACTIVITIES

1. If $\frac{1}{3}$ of the people at the event were male, how many were female?

_____

2. How good is your sense of balance? Stand on one leg with your eyes closed. For how many seconds can you hold it?

_____

3. For how many seconds can you balance this book on your head?

_____

120

Most People Sitting on One Chair

Photo: Guinness World Records Limited

At Springfield Secondary School in Singapore, 1,058 people sat on one chair on August 16, 2008.

Did You Know?

In Lipan, Texas, you can visit the Star of Texas Rocker. It's a 26-ft.-tall cedar log rocking chair.

ACTIVITIES

1. How many chairs would be needed at the event if only 46 people could sit on one chair?

   _____

2. How many friends and family members can sit on one chair at your house?

   _____

3. How many different chairs have you sat in today?

   _____

Photo: Guinness World Records Limited

In Lisbon, Portugal, on June 5, 2010, 15,956 people wore red noses.

Did You Know?

The event was organized to bring attention to a charitable group that sends clowns to visit hospitalized children in Portugal.

ACTIVITIES

1. If each person at the event gave $2.00 to a charity, how much money would the charity collect?

_____

2. Circle jobs at the circus you would like to try.

acrobat	clown	trapeze artist
tightrope walker	lion tamer	juggler
ringmaster	contortionist	fire eater

Most People Treading Grapes

Photo: Guinness World Records Limited

Nine hundred seventy-seven people stomped on grapes in Labastida, Álava, Spain, on September 25, 2010.

Did You Know?

For the record-setting attempt, 28 tons of grapes were used and 3,849 gallons of juice were squeezed.

ACTIVITIES

1. The record was set in a town in the Basque Country in northern Spain. Look at a map. What mountain range is found in that same region near the French border?

_____

2. Some wine makers think juice from grapes stomped by bare human feet tastes better than juice pressed by machine. What cooking tasks do you like to do best with your own hands?

_____

Most People Twirling Lassos Simultaneously

Photo: Guinness World Records Limited

Sixty-nine people twirled lassos simultaneously at the Campeonato Nacional Charro in Guadalajara, Mexico, on September 4, 2010.

Did You Know?
Some participants simply twirled the lassos, but many performed *floreando la soga*, or trick roping.

ACTIVITIES

1. Charros and cowboys use ropes in their work. In what other professions and hobbies are ropes used?

   _____

2. Use a book or a Web site to help you learn to tie one knot. Useful knots include square knots, clove hitch, and figure eight. Write the name of the knot you learned and explain how to do it.

   _____

   _____

Photo: Guinness World Records Limited

ULTIMATE FOODS

Photo: Guinness World Records Limited

Largest Jawbreaker

Photo: Guinness World Records Limited

A jawbreaker with a circumference of 37.25 in. (94.6 cm) and weighing 27.8 lb. (12.6 kg) was made in Scarborough, Ontario, Canada. It took 476 hours to make it between January 7 and May 29, 2003.

Did You Know?

A *jawbreaker* is a hard candy that can be as large as a golf ball or as small as a candy sprinkle. It takes more than two weeks to make a jawbreaker!

ACTIVITIES

British people know jawbreakers as *gobstoppers*. Match British and American words.

British	American
biscuit	truck
lift	suspicious
wardrobe	elevator
dodgy	cookie
mate	closet
lorry	friend

Most Ice Cream Scoops Thrown and Caught in One Minute by a Team of Two

Photo: Guinness World Records Limited

On September 1, 2007, in Cologne, Germany, Gabriele Soravia and Lorenzo Soravia (both Germany) threw and caught 25 scoops of ice cream in one minute.

Did You Know?
You have to lick a one-scoop ice cream cone about 50 times to make it disappear.

ACTIVITIES

1. The team caught 25 scoops in one minute. How many scoops could they catch in 5.5 minutes? Round to the nearest whole number.

   _____

2. People love to invent ice cream flavors like brownie batter or peanut butter and jelly. Invent a new ice cream flavor.

   _____

3. How many times can you throw and catch stuffed animals with a friend in one minute?

   _____

Largest Curry

Photo: Guinness World Records Limited

The largest serving of curry was made on July 16, 2005, by Abdul Salam (UK) and weighed 22,707.61 lb. (10.3 metric tons).

Did You Know?

The earliest known recipe for meat in spicy sauce was found on a stone tablet dated around 1700 BC.

ACTIVITIES

1. Curry is a mix of meat and vegetables in a spicy sauce. What is your favorite spicy food?

   _____

2. Many people in India love curry. Look at a map. What large mountain range is north of India?

   _____

3. The largest curry weighed 22,707 pounds. What number is in the hundreds place?

   _____

Most Meatballs Eaten in One Minute

Photo: Guinness World Records Limited

Takeru Kobayashi (Japan) ate 29 meatballs in one minute on March 8, 2010, in Brooklyn, New York.

Did You Know?

People have been eating meatballs for a long time. An 1877 meatball recipe called for meat from calf and sheep necks.

ACTIVITIES

1. In one minute, 29 meatballs were eaten. At that rate, how many could be eaten in 26 minutes?

_____

2. What's your favorite pasta to eat with meatballs? Draw the shape of each type of pasta next to its name.

fusilli   **macaroni**

tortellini   **spaghetti**

Most Expensive Pizza

Photo: Guinness World Records Limited

At a restaurant in London, United Kingdom, a pizza topped with fresh shavings of a white truffle sells for $178. A white truffle is a rare Italian edible fungus worth $2,500 for 2 lb. 3 oz. (1 kg).

Did You Know?

The most popular pizza topping in the U.S. is pepperoni. In Japan, the most popular pizza topping is squid!

CHECK THIS OUT!

Pizza is usually tasty and fairly inexpensive. At some restaurants, you can get a whole pizza for only $5. But, one restaurant in London, called *Maze*, broke the record for creating the world's Most Expensive Pizza. Each pizza sells for $178!

This gourmet pizza has a thin crust and is topped with onions, mushrooms, and two types of cheese. So, what makes this pizza so special and expensive? It is topped with wild lettuce and shavings of white truffle, a rare fungus. Truffles are hard to find, which makes them very expensive. The white truffle used on this pizza costs about $1,000 per pound! Would you trade a cheese pizza for a fungus pizza at any price?

1. How much would you spend before taxes and tip at Maze to buy each person in a family of four a record-breaking pizza?

   a. $712

   b. $1,000

   c. $20

   d. $178

2. An average tip at a nice restaurant is 20 percent. About how much should you leave as a tip for purchasing one record-breaking pizza? Circle your answer.

   more than $30   **less than $30**

3. The world's Most Expensive Hamburger (page 165) is sold for $186. Is it more or less expensive than the world's Most Expensive Pizza? Write <, >, or = to complete the equation.

   $186 ◯ $178

4. The world's Most Expensive Sandwich (page 144) is sold for $200. How much money could you save by buying the record-breaking pizza instead of the record-breaking sandwich?

   _____

5. Pretend you have $200 to spend on food for one meal. What would you do with it? Would you want to buy the record-breaking hamburger, pizza, or sandwich? Explain your answer.

   _____

   _____

   _____

   _____

   _____

   _____

   _____

Largest Scrambled Eggs

Photo: Guinness World Records Limited

On December 1, 2009, scrambled eggs weighing 2,733 lb. 11 oz. (1,240 kg) were made in Cathedral Square, Christchurch, New Zealand. More than 20,000 eggs and 26.4 gal. (100 L) of cream were used to make the eggs.

Did You Know?

A chicken farm in Ohio has 4.8 million hens that lay about 3.7 million eggs—every day!

ACTIVITIES

1. How do you like to eat eggs for breakfast?

   _____

2. About 20,000 eggs were used for this record. What is $\frac{1}{10}$ of 20,000?

   _____

3. If a gallon of cream costs $10, how much would 26.5 gallons of cream cost?

   _____

Hamburger Stuffing

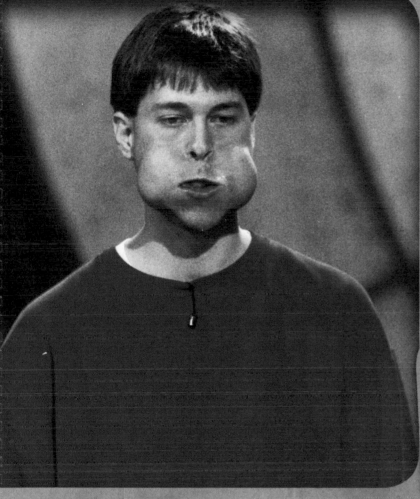

Photo: Guinness World Records Limited

On June 17, 1998, Johnny Reitz (USA) stuffed three regulation-size hamburgers (including buns and condiments) into his mouth on the set of *Guinness World Records: Primetime*.

Did you Know?

Food contests are popular. People compete to eat the most hot dogs, pizza, ice cream, pie, cake, corn on the cob, and other foods.

ACTIVITIES

1. Circle toppings you like to eat on a hamburger or veggie burger.

lettuce	pickles	cheese
ketchup	mustard	onions
mayonnaise	bacon	mushrooms

2. Have a contest with a friend. How many soft toys can each of you stuff into a backpack? What was the winning record?

_____

Largest Bagel

Photo: Guinness World Records Limited

On August 27, 2004, Brueggers Bagels (USA) presented an 868 lb. (393.7 kg) bagel at the New York State Fair in Geddes, New York.

Did You Know?

Mattoon, Illinois, claims to be the bagel capital of the world. Each summer, they host a bagel festival, where more than 60,000 bagels are eaten.

ACTIVITIES

1. People like bagels with cream cheese, butter, peanut butter, jam, or lox. What is your favorite way to eat a bagel?

   _____

2. Bagels are the only type of bread that is boiled. What else is cooked in boiling water?

   _____

3. Some bagel varieties are cinnamon-raisin, cranberry-vanilla, and "everything." Invent a new bagel and write its name.

   _____

Most People Tossing Pancakes

Photo: Guinness World Records Limited

On October 24, 2008, during a television show attempt for Guinness World Records Day in Almere, Netherlands, 405 people simultaneously tossed pancakes in the air.

Did You Know?

A pancake has also been called a *flapjack, flapcake, flapover, flipjack, flopover, griddlecake, hotcake, flannel cake,* and a *slapjack.*

ACTIVITIES

1. How do you think the pancake got its name?

   _____

2. If 12 people each ordered a stack of six pancakes at a restaurant, how many pancakes would there be in all?

   _____

3. Write the name of a breakfast food you can make for yourself.

   _____

Largest Ice Cream Cup

Photo: Guinness World Records Limited

A 6 ft. 5 in. (1.96 m) tall cup of ice cream was presented on September 13, 2005, in Canton, Massachusetts. It weighed 8,865 lb. (4,021 kg).

Did You Know?

More ice cream is bought on Sunday than on any other day of the week.

CHECK THIS OUT!

Anniversaries are special days. Sometimes, people celebrate in unusual ways. In 2005, an ice cream company had its 60th anniversary and wanted to celebrate by breaking a record for the world's Largest Ice Cream Cup. The ice cream cup took 1,289 gallons of vanilla ice cream and weighed 8,865 pounds. It weighed as much as three cars!

Breaking the record was not easy. First, people had to make a giant cup and scoop ice cream into it. Six people scooped for 15 hours. Then, the whole thing had to be weighed quickly, before the ice cream started to melt!

Two people measured the mound of ice cream. It took 20 minutes to get all of the measurements. Finally, the record was confirmed! By then, there was only one thing left to do, so everyone grabbed a spoon and began to eat!

1. Why did the company want to set a world record?

_____

2. What does *confirmed* mean? Why is it important that a world record is confirmed?

_____

_____

3. Circle five words you read on page 136 to complete the word search. Use the word bank to help you.

> ice cream   scoop   cup   vanilla   celebrate

```
G  R  V  H  T  H  E  O  I
H  E  A  V  A  W  H  I  C
L  K  N  L  P  D  S  C  E
A  X  I  C  W  H  K  U  C
R  U  L  S  C  O  O  P  R
C  E  L  E  B  R  A  T  E
Z  Q  A  A  C  R  V  Y  A
J  T  E  Y  R  F  G  L  M
```

4. You should always do something special on an anniversary. Do you agree with this statement? Explain why or why not.

_____

_____

_____

Longest Line of Pizzas

Photo: Guinness World Records Limited

On May 16, 2009, the Van Duzer Foundation and the St. Lucie County Education Foundation (both USA) assembled a 1,777 ft. 7 in. (541.8 m) line of 12 in. (30.48 cm) pizzas. It took 1,800 pizzas to make the line in Fort Pierce, Florida.

Did You Know?

A pizza made in Madrid, Spain, was hand-delivered 12,347 mi. (19,870 km) away in Wellington, New Zealand.

ACTIVITIES

1. What number is in the thousands place in 1,800?

_____

2. Draw lines to divide these pizzas so that five people can each have four slices.

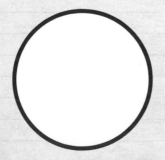  

Largest Jug of Soft Drink

Photo: Guinness World Records Limited

On June 8, 2008, in Olinda, Pernambuco, Brazil, the jug measured 11 ft. 11 in. (3.38 m) tall and had a circumference of 25 ft. 10 in. (7.87 m). It was filled with 2,456.8 gal. (9,300 L) of soft drink.

Did You Know?

In 1886, Dr. John Pemberton cooked up the first Coca-Cola recipe in a kettle in his backyard. It first sold for five cents a glass!

ACTIVITIES

1. The jug was filled with 2,456 gallons of soft drink. How many more gallons would make it 2,800?

_____

2. When soda pop loses its carbonation and is no longer full of carbon dioxide, it is "flat." Let a cup of soda go flat, then weigh it on a scale. Now, weigh the same amount of fizzy soda. What did you find out?

_____

_____

Most Rice Eaten With Chopsticks in Three Minutes

On November 9, 2007, in Ocean Gate, New Jersey, Rob Beaton (USA) ate 78 grains of rice with chopsticks, one by one, in three minutes.

Did You Know?
There are more than 29,000 grains of rice in a 1 lb. (453 g) bag of long grain rice.

Photo: Guinness World Records Limited

ACTIVITIES

1. To make beginner chopsticks, wrap a rubber band tightly around the back ends to bind them together. Wedge a folded-up scrap of paper between them, just under the rubber band. Now, practice picking up small items. How did you do?

_____

2. How many grains of rice or pieces of cereal can you pick up in three minutes?

_____

Largest Pretzel

Photo: Guinness World Records Limited

Olaf Kluyand and Manfred Keilwerth (both Germany) baked a pretzel weighing 842 lb. (382 kg). It measured 26 ft. 11 in. (8.2 m) long and 10 ft. 2 in. (3.1 m) wide on September 21, 2008, in Neufahrn, Germany.

Did You Know?

It is said that hard pretzels were discovered in the 1600s when a baker's apprentice fell asleep and let the pretzels bake too long.

ACTIVITIES

1. Read above to find out the length and width of the Largest Pretzel. Would it fit inside the room you are in right now? Circle your answer.

   yes   no

2. The pretzel weighed 842 pounds. A refrigerator weighs about 200 pounds. Write < or > to complete the statement.

   Largest Pretzel ◯ 3 refrigerators

3. What is your favorite salty snack?

Largest Pancake

Photo: Guinness World Records Limited

On August 13, 1994, it took four hours to cook an enormous two-million-calorie pancake in Rochdale, Greater Manchester, United Kingdom. It measured 49 ft. 3 in. (15.01 m) in diameter, 1 in. (2.5 cm) thick, and weighed 6,614 lb. (3 metric tons).

Did You Know?

Aunt Jemima pancake flour, the first ready-mix food, was invented in 1899. It was made at a flour mill in St. Joseph, Missouri.

CHECK THIS OUT!

Nothing starts the day off better than a well-balanced breakfast. Studies show that eating breakfast every day is important in maintaining a healthy weight. It can even help you do better in school! Pancakes, when combined with fruit, juice, or milk, can be a part of a healthy breakfast.

Do you like pancakes? If you do, you would flip over this one! In 1994, some people in Manchester, United Kingdom, cooked a huge pancake, the largest in the world! It took 5,966.4 pounds of pancake mix and 1,074.7 gallons of water to make the batter. The pancake cooked for four hours in a pan that was 50 feet wide. This record-setting pancake had a whopping two million calories. If the average adult should consume 2,000 calories per day, this pancake could feed 1,000 people!

ACTIVITIES

1. What is the radius of the pan in which the world's Largest Pancake
was cooked?

_____

2. Arrange these numbers in order from least to greatest.

   5,966.4   **1,074.7**   **2,000,000**   **6,614**

   _____   _____   _____   _____

3. The world's Largest Cinnamon Roll weighed 246.5 pounds. Which equation
would you use to find how much more the world's Largest Pancake weighed
than the world's Largest Cinnamon Roll? (Hint: n equals the difference
in weight.)

   a. $6{,}614 \div n = 246.5$

   b. $6{,}614 - 246.5 = n$

   c. $246.5 \times n = 6{,}614$

   d. $n - 246.5 = 6{,}614$

4. What is the answer to the equation you chose in #3?

_____

5. What do you usually eat for breakfast? What are some things you could change to
make it healthier?

_____

_____

6. What are some objects that are the same shape as a pancake? Draw them here.

Most Expensive Sandwich

Photo: Guinness World Records Limited

The von Essen Platinum Club Sandwich is available at a restaurant in Buckinghamshire, United Kingdom, for $200. The sandwich was added to the menu in March 2007.

Did You Know?

This sandwich contained special kinds of ham, chicken, truffles, quail eggs, and dried tomatoes packed between three slices of sourdough bread.

ACTIVITIES

1. The sandwich costs $200. How many $10 bills would you need to pay?

_____

2. How many $20 bills would you need to pay?

_____

3. Write four ingredients you would use to create a tasty sandwich.

_____   _____

_____   _____

Largest Candy Mosaic

Photo: Guinness World Records Limited

On October 18, 2009, students, children, and volunteers joined together to create a candy mosaic in Madrid, Spain. It was 853 sq. ft. (79.32 m²) and consisted of 150,000 pieces of candy.

Did You Know?
Before the first chewing gum was made, people chewed tree resin to freshen their breath.

ACTIVITIES

A mosaic is a picture made from tiny pieces. Color squares in different colors to make a mosaic.

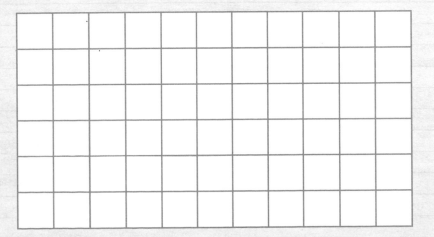

Fastest Time to Eat a 12-Inch Pizza

Photo: Guinness World Records Limited

On March 22, 2008, Josh Anderson (New Zealand) ate a 12 in. (30.48 cm) pizza in 1 minute 45.37 seconds.

Did You Know?
The first mozzarella cheese was made from the milk of a water buffalo!

ACTIVITIES

1. Anderson ate one pizza in about $1\frac{3}{4}$ minutes. About how many pizzas could he eat in five minutes? Round to the nearest whole number.

_____

2. Circle your favorite pizza toppings.

chicken	**mushrooms**	**pepperoni**
pineapple	**peppers**	**sausage**
onions	**spinach**	**tomatoes**

Largest Paella

Photo: Guinness World Records Limited

On March 8, 1992, in Valencia, Spain, 100,000 people ate paella that measured 65 ft. 7 in. (20 m) in diameter. Paella is a saffron-flavored dish containing rice, meat, seafood, and vegetables.

Did You Know?

The marsh rat was one of the main ingredients of the first paellas, along with eel and beans.

ACTIVITIES

1. The paella served 100,000 people. If 10,000 people ate each hour, how many hours would it take to serve everyone?

   _____

2. Look at a map. What continent is just below the country of Spain?

   _____

3. What is the capital of Spain?

   _____

Most Worms Eaten (30 Seconds)

Photo: Guinness World Records Limited

On November 15, 2003, C. Manoharan "Snake" Manu (India) swallowed 200 earthworms, each measuring at least 4 in. (10 cm) long, in 30 seconds. He ate the worms in Chennai City, Tamil Nadu, India.

Did You Know?
A *Wormzel* is a pretzel made from worms that have been cleaned, tied in a knot, and cooked. They are said to be delicious when served with mustard.

CHECK THIS OUT!

What is the strangest thing that you have ever eaten? Squid? Caviar? Frog legs? "Snake" Manu (India), as he likes to be called, has eaten insects, lizards, and snakes. He began experimenting as an eight-year-old, performing strange tricks to amuse his classmates.

At age 18, Manu found his specialty. He put a half-dead water snake into his nose and pulled it out of his mouth. This trick is what Manu calls *snake flossing.* Since then, he has tried all kinds of live snakes. His favorites are small cobras because they are flexible, but he has also used kraits, sand boas, and rat snakes. One time, a snake got stuck in his throat. Manu had to choose between biting the snake or being bitten by it. After that, he started eating the snakes that he inserted through his nose!

ACTIVITIES

1. Earthworms can be a good source of protein. Research different types of foods that provide protein for our bodies. Create a menu that features these food items. Include an appetizer, a main course, and a dessert.

Menu

_____

_____

_____

_____

_____

2. What types of things has Manu eaten?

   a. squid, insects, and snakes

   b. frog legs, caviar, and snakes

   c. lizards, insects, and snakes

   d. squid, frog legs, and caviar

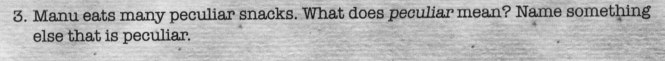

3. Manu eats many peculiar snacks. What does *peculiar* mean? Name something else that is peculiar.

_____

_____

4. What is the most likely reason Manu started performing these tricks?

   a. He likes the taste of the strange snacks.

   b. He likes the attention that he gets from performing such daring acts.

   c. He likes handling dangerous snakes.

   d. He gets bored easily.

Largest Smoothie

Photo: Guinness World Records Limited

On July 8, 2010, in Toronto, Ontario, Canada, a 264.17-gal. (1,000-L) blueberry smoothie was made. It contained 145.29 gal. (550 L) of milk and 39.63 gal. (150 L) of yogurt.

Did You Know?

This smoothie was sweetened with 9.25 gal. (35 L) of honey and 661.39 lb. (300 kg) of blueberries.

ACTIVITIES

1. Write what fruits and ingredients you would choose to make a nutritious and delicious smoothie.

   _____

2. Blueberries are blue! Write a favorite food that matches each color.

   red: _____

   white: _____

   brown: _____

   yellow: _____

Most Noodle Strings Made

Photo: Guinness World Records Limited

Hiroshi Kuroda (Japan) made 65,536 noodle strings in one minute using only 16 movements on November 28, 2009, in Nasushiobara, Tochigi, Japan.

Did You Know?

In Japan, noisily slurping noodles is not considered bad manners, but a sign that you are enjoying your meal!

ACTIVITIES

1. What can you do in 16 movements? Can you pour a cold drink or get dressed?

   _____

2. Your brain is sometimes called your *noodle*. Write two more words that can mean "brain."

   _____   _____

3. Noodles are eaten around the world. What is your favorite noodle dish?

   _____

Largest Bowl of Cereal

Photo: Guinness World Records Limited

On July 2, 2007, a bowl of cereal weighing 2,204 lb. 10 oz. (1,000 kg) was made in Johannesburg, South Africa. The bowl was 4 ft. 11 in. (1.5 m) tall with a diameter of 8 ft. 6 in. (2.6 m).

Did You Know?

There are approximately 299 Rice Krispies in a Rice Krispies bar.

ACTIVITIES

Cereal-only restaurants let customers mix and match different cereals and toppings. Make a sign for your own cereal restaurant. Explain what is on your menu.

Most Grapes Caught in the Mouth in Three Minutes

Photo: Guinness World Records Limited

Ashrita Furman (USA) caught 182 grapes in his mouth in three minutes at the Grand Canyon National Park, Arizona, on July 10, 2009. He caught the grapes from a distance of 15 ft. (1.57 m).

Did You Know?
The farthest a marshmallow has been blown out of one person's nostril and into the mouth of another is 16 ft. 3.3 in. (4.96 m).

ACTIVITIES

1. Have a friend toss a grape or a piece of cereal. Can you catch it in your mouth? Circle your answer.

   yes   **no**

2. Stand about 15 feet away from a friend. What can you catch from that distance?

   _____

3. The Grand Canyon is a national park in Arizona. What national park is closest to your home?

   _____

Largest Rabbit Made of Chocolate

Photo: Guinness World Records Limited

On March 19, 2010, in Sandton City, Gauten, South Africa, a giant chocolate rabbit weighed 6,635.91 lb. (3,010 kg) and measured 12 ft. 6 in. (3.8 m) tall.

Did You Know?

Chocolate is made from seeds found in cacao tree pods. One pod contains 30–50 seeds, enough to make seven milk chocolate candy bars!

CHECK THIS OUT!

Most people like bunnies. Most people also like chocolate. So, it makes sense to put the two together. In fact, each year about 90 million chocolate bunnies are made. In 2009, a company made a huge chocolate rabbit weighing more than 6,000 pounds! The bunny weighed one-and-a-half times as much as a car!

The first chocolate bunny was made 200 years ago in Germany. The bunny was made to celebrate spring. Later, some people from Germany moved to the United States and brought their love of chocolate bunnies with them. Soon, people in the United States were eating chocolate bunnies. Some were milk chocolate, some were dark chocolate, and some were white chocolate.

1. Find Germany and South Africa on a map. On what continents are these two countries? About how many miles separate them?

_____

_____

2. How do you eat a chocolate rabbit? One study found that 91 percent of Americans think you should eat the ears first. Do you agree? Explain why or why not.

_____

_____

3. Chocolate rabbits have been around for 400 years. True or false? Circle your answer.

true   **false**

4. Chocolate rabbits were originally made to celebrate spring. What other ways do people celebrate spring?

_____

_____

5. Conduct a survey of your friends and family to find out their favorite kinds of chocolate. How many like dark chocolate best, how many like milk chocolate best, and how many like white chocolate best? How many do not like chocolate at all? Make a chart to display your results.

Highest Dinner Party

Photo: Guinness World Records Limited

On May 3, 2004, eight people, including an appointed butler, dined in formal clothing at 22,326 ft. (6,805 m) on Lhakpa Ri, Tibet.

Did You Know?

The food for this party included caviar, duck, chocolate bombe, cheese, and birthday cake.

ACTIVITIES

1. If you could have your next birthday party anywhere in the world, where would it be?

   _____

2. If each table seats eight people, how many tables would 104 people need?

   _____

3. Who would you invite to a fancy dinner?

   _____

Largest Popcorn Ball

Photo: Guinness World Records Limited.

A popcorn ball weighed 3,423 lb. (1,552.64 kg) on September 29, 2005, in Lake Forest, Illinois.

Did You Know?

There are six kinds of corn, but only the kernels of popcorn pop. They can pop as high as 3 ft. (91 cm) in the air!

ACTIVITIES

1. How many more pounds would be needed to make the popcorn ball 5,000 pounds?

_____

2. An *onomatopoeia* is a word that copies a sound. The word *pop* is one example. Circle more examples.

apple	zip	splash
meow	think	boom
clap	green	knock

Strangest Diet

Photo: Guinness World Records Limited

Since 1966, Michel Lotito (France) has eaten 18 bicycles, 15 shopping carts, seven televisions, six chandeliers, two beds, a pair of skis, a Cessna light aircraft, and a computer. He first learned of his unusual ability when his drinking glass broke and he began chewing the pieces.

Did You Know?
Lotito can eat grocery carts and bicycles, but says that eating bananas and hard-boiled eggs makes him sick!

ACTIVITIES

1. How many wheels do 18 bicycles have?

_____

2. Do you love carrots or toast with jam? What food have you eaten three times or more in the past week?

_____

3. How many items did Lotito eat in all?

_____

Largest Serving of French Fries

Photo: Guinness World Records Limited

On February 19, 2004, an 812.4 lb. (368.5 kg) bag of French fries was made at the Hereford Racecourse in Hereford, United Kingdom.

Did You Know?

During the Potato Bowl USA in 2006, about 10,000 people ate 4,621 lb. (2,096 kg) of French fries with 113 gal. (428 L) of ketchup.

ACTIVITIES

1. If one potato makes 15 French fries, how many fries could you make from six potatoes?

   _____

2. With adult help, make healthy oven fries. Coat potato wedges with olive oil and some salt. Bake in a 450°F oven for 15–20 minutes. How did your fries taste?

   _____

Largest Cupcake

On October 3, 2009, a cupcake weighing 1,315 lb. (596.47 kg) was presented at the second annual Think Pink Rocks charity concert in Boca Raton, Florida.

Photo: Guinness World Records Limited

Did You Know?

Long ago, some people called cupcakes *number cakes* because early recipes read: 1 cup of butter, 2 cups of sugar, 3 cups of flour, and so on.

CHECK THIS OUT!

What weighed 1,315 pounds, holds a Guinness World Record, and would satisfy anyone's sweet tooth? The world's Largest Cupcake! This cupcake broke the world record at a charity concert in Boca Raton, Florida.

The recipe for this sweet treat called for an amazing 340 pounds of sugar, 346 pounds of eggs, and 75 pounds of butter! After the bakers mixed all of the ingredients together and baked the cupcake for 24 hours, it was ready to be measured. The chocolate-flavored dessert measured a jaw-dropping 6 feet wide and 4.5 feet tall!

ACTIVITIES

1. How much would the world's Largest Cupcake weigh if the recipe were tripled?

_____

2. If the world's Largest Cupcake recipe were doubled, how many pounds of eggs would be needed for the recipe?

   a. 346

   b. 692

   c. 150

   d. 680

3. Rank these sweet treats in your order of preference.

   Cupcakes   **Cookies**   **Brownies**   **Candy Bars**

   _____   _____   _____   _____

4. Unscramble words you read on page 160.

   gegs _____   **rgusa** _____

   etwes _____   **eutbrt** _____

   eciepr _____   **kuccpea** _____

5. The world's Largest Cheesecake (page 164) topped the scales at a whopping 4,704 pounds! How much more did the cheesecake weigh over the cupcake?

_____

6. Circle something in each category to describe your favorite cupcake.

   Cake Flavor: **Icing:**   **With:**

   chocolate   chocolate   sprinkles

   yellow   vanilla   a cherry

   red velvet   peanut butter   chocolate syrup

Tallest Stack of Pancakes

Photo: Guinness World Records Limited

On August 26, 2008, Krunoslav Budiselic (Croatia) made a 2 ft. 5 in. (74 cm) tall stack of pancakes at a hotel in Terme Catez, Slovenia.

Did You Know?

Many people pour maple syrup on their pancakes. Maple syrup is made from the tree sap found in maple trees.

ACTIVITIES

1. Make a stack of blocks, books, or other non-breakable items that is two feet, five inches tall. Write what you stacked.

_____

2. Cut circles from paper to make pancake cards. With a friend, write numbers and symbols on the cards to make a game. Write the name of your game and one of the rules.

_____

_____

Largest Bag of Potato Chips

Photo. Guinness World Records Limited

On March 11, 2004, the largest bag of potato chips was made in Bradford, West Yorkshire, United Kingdom. It weighed 113 lb. 7 oz. (51.35 kg).

Did You Know?
A couple hundred years ago, potatoes were served for dessert!

ACTIVITIES

1. How many more ounces of potato chips would be needed for a 115-pound bag?

   _____

2. At $2.25 per bag, how much would three bags of chips cost?

   _____

3. Baked, mashed, or fried? What is your favorite way to eat potatoes?

   _____

Largest Cheesecake

Photo: Guinness World Records Limited

On January 25, 2009, in Mexico City, Mexico, a cheesecake was made measuring 1 ft. 10 in. (56 cm) tall, with a diameter of 8 ft. 2 in. (2.5 m). It weighed 4,704 lb. (2,133.5 kg).

Did You Know?

To make this giant cheesecake, they mixed 1,763.7 lb. (800 kg) of cheese with an equal amount of yogurt!

ACTIVITIES

1. Give the height of the Largest Cheesecake in inches.

   _____

2. Write *cake* to complete each word.

   cup_____   cheese_____

   pan _____   _____walk

   short_____   fruit_____

Most Expensive Hamburger

Photo: Guinness World Records Limited

A limited-edition hamburger, called "The Burger," was on the menu at a Burger King in London, United Kingdom, for $186 on June 18, 2008.

Did You Know?

In 1948, a hamburger at the first McDonald's restaurant cost 15 cents!

ACTIVITIES

1. How much would it cost if each person in a family of four ordered the Most Expensive Hamburger?

_____

2. Circle a number to show how much you like to eat hamburgers.

1	2	3	4	5
Yuck!		**OK**		**Yum!**

3. How much do you like to eat bananas?

1	2	3	4	5
Yuck!		**OK**		**Yum!**

Largest Collection of Banana-Related Memorabilia

Photo: Guinness World Records Limited

Ken Bannister (USA) is the owner of the International Banana Club Museum in Altadena, California. He has 17,000 banana-related items and has been collecting since 1972.

Did You Know?
The inside of a banana peel is good for polishing patent leather shoes.

CHECK THIS OUT!

Ken Bannister (United States) is bananas for bananas. He is known as "Banana Man," and he owns 17,000 banana items.

Bannister began his quest in 1972. He handed out banana stickers for a fruit company. When he ran out of stickers, he made some of his own. These stickers were for the International Banana Club.

Soon, Bannister had an idea. He would offer degrees in Bananistry to people who sent him banana items. Eventually, Bannister had tons of items and decided to start a museum. The International Banana Club Museum opened in California in 1976.

Today, the Banana Club has members in 17 countries. Bannister says the purpose of the club is to make people smile. Anyone can join!

ACTIVITIES

1. When did Bannister begin collecting banana items?

   a. 1972

   b. 1976

   c. 1927

   d. 1967

2. How many countries are represented in the International Banana Club? Circle your answer.

   more than 15   **less than 15**

3. What does *quest* mean? Write your own sentence using that word.

   _____

   _____

4. Read the following statements. Circle *true* or *false*.

   Bannister is known as "Banana Kid."   true   false

   Anyone can join the Banana Club.   true   false

   The museum is in California.   true   false

5. Bannister designed his own sticker for the International Banana Club. Design and draw a sticker for a club that you create.

Largest Wedding Cake

Photo: Guinness World Records Limited

A New England bridal showcase in Uncasville, Connecticut, displayed a wedding cake weighing 15,031 lb. (6.82 metric tons) on February 8, 2004.

Did You Know?

In ancient Rome, they broke a cake over the bride's head to wish her a life of abundance! Sometimes, they ate the crumbs for good luck!

ACTIVITIES

Make the cake weigh a total of 28 pounds. Write how many pounds each cake tier should weigh.

_____ pounds

_____ pounds

_____ pounds

_____ pounds

_____ pounds

Largest Steak Commercially Available

Photo: Guinness World Records Limited

At a restaurant in Hatton, Derbyshire, United Kingdom, you can order a steak that weighs 12.5 lb. (5.67 kg) before it is cooked. It costs about $185 and includes the side dish of your choice.

Did You Know?
It takes about 40 minutes to cook this steak to "medium-well" on a huge grill. No one has ever been able to eat the entire slab of meat!

ACTIVITIES

1. Some restaurants challenge their customers to eat the largest sandwich or the hottest pepper on the menu. What food challenge would you make if you had a restaurant?

_____

_____

2. The largest steak weighs about 12 pounds raw. If it loses $\frac{1}{4}$ of its weight during cooking, how much does it weigh when served?

_____

Largest Hot Cross Bun

Photo: Guinness World Records Limited

The largest hot cross bun was made on April 4, 2009, in Capetown, South Africa, and weighed 227.08 lb. (103 kg).

Did You Know?

A grandmother in the United Kingdom owns a hot cross bun that was baked in 1821, nearly 200 years ago!

ACTIVITIES

1. Does the Largest Hot Cross Bun weigh more or less than the Largest Bag of Potato Chips on page 163? Circle your answer.

   more   **less**

2. Sharing a hot cross bun is said to bond friends, especially if they say, "Half for you and half for me, between us two shall goodwill be." Write what you shared with a friend.

   _____

   _____

Largest Prawn/Shrimp Cocktail

Photo: Guinness World Records Limited

On July 10, 2009, in London, United Kingdom, a 219.84 lb.(99.72 kg) glass of shrimp cocktail was served in a cocktail glass that measured 4 ft. 11 in. (1.5 m) tall

Did You Know?

A shrimp's head is half of its body size, and its heart is located in its head!

ACTIVITIES

1. If you need $1\frac{1}{2}$ dozen shrimp for a recipe, how many shrimp should you buy?

_____

2. Ask five people to tell their favorite kind of seafood. Color spaces in the graph to show your results.

fish					
shrimp					
crab					
lobster					

Largest Pizza Base Spun in Two Minutes

Photo: Guinness World Records Limited

On April 20, 2006, in Minneapolis, Minnesota, Tony Gemignani (USA) spun 1 lb. 2 oz. (500 g) of dough for two minutes to form a pizza base that measured 2 ft. 9.2 in. (84.33 cm) wide.

Did You Know?
The world's Highest Pizza Toss is 21 ft. 5 in.

CHECK THIS OUT!

Around and around the pizza maker tosses the dough. At a pizzeria, a large pizza is usually 16 inches in diameter. Tony Gemignani (United States), though, spun a pizza base more than twice that size! The Largest Pizza Base Spun in Two Minutes contained 17.6 ounces of dough and had a diameter of 33.2 inches. That's one big pizza!

However, that pizza doesn't even compare to the world's Largest Pizza. This pizza, made in South Africa in December 1990, weighed 26,874 pounds! To make the pizza, bakers used 9,920 pounds of flour, 198 pounds of salt, 198 pounds of yeast, 772 gallons of water, 1,984 pounds of tomato puree, 1,984 pounds of chopped tomatoes, 3,968 pounds of cheese, and 396 pounds of margarine! The preparation and cooking of the pizza took about 39 hours.

ACTIVITIES

1. How many seconds are there in two minutes?

   a. 60

   b. 90

   c. 120

   d. 150

2. If one ordinary pizza weighs 2.7 pounds, about how many ordinary pizzas would it take to equal the weight of the world's Largest Pizza?

   _____

3. Complete the crossword puzzle with words you read on page 172.

   Across

   2. The world's Largest Pizza used 9,920 pounds of _____ .

   4. The world's Largest Pizza used 3,968 pounds of _____ .

   5. A _____ pizza is usually 16 inches in diameter.

   6. The world's Largest Pizza was made here.

   7. Place where you can order a pizza for dinner

   Down

   1. He holds the record for the Largest Pizza Base Spun in Two Minutes.

   3. State where Tony Gemignani set his world record

Largest Potato Gratin

Photo: Guinness World Records Limited

The largest potato gratin measured 32 ft. 9 in. (10 m) by 6 ft. 6 in. (2 m). It was prepared on January 29, 2010, in Alpe d'Huez, France. It weighed 6,636 lb. (3,010 kg) and was made with 2,700 potatoes, 661 lb. (300 kg) of cream, and 22 lb. (10 kg) of garlic.

Did You Know?

There is a Potato Museum in Washington, D.C., which has over 2,000 potato artifacts.

ACTIVITIES

1. If garlic is sold in two-pound bags, how many bags would be needed for the Largest Potato Gratin?

_____

2. Warm potato gratin tastes good on a cold day. What food do you like to eat on a cold day?

_____

3. Where do potatoes grow? Circle your answer.

above ground   **underground**

Fastest Time to Eat a Bowl of Pasta

Photo: Guinness World Records Limited

On November 12, 2009, Ernesto Cesario (Italy) ate a bowl of pasta in 1 minute 30 seconds. The pasta and sauce weighed 5.3 oz. (150 g).

Did You Know?

President Thomas Jefferson bought a machine for making macaroni in Italy and helped to make macaroni and cheese famous in the United States.

ACTIVITIES

1. How many seconds did it take Cesario to eat the bowl of pasta?

_____

2. Did the bowl of pasta weigh more or less than $\frac{1}{2}$ pound? Circle your answer.

   more   **less**

3. What is your favorite kind of pasta sauce?

_____

Largest Chocolate (Individual)

Photo: Guinness World Records Limited

On July 7, 2007, at Chocolate World, Hershey, Pennsylvania, a giant Hershey's Kiss weighing 30,540 lb. (13,852.71 kg) was displayed to celebrate the 100th anniversary of Hershey's Kisses.

Did You Know?

Some reports say the Aztec king, Montezuma, drank 50 glasses of chocolate a day!

ACTIVITIES

1. The Largest Chocolate was made to celebrate a 100th anniversary. Color enough 10s to equal 100.

2. Do you like hot chocolate? Chocolate bars? Chocolate pudding? Tell your favorite way to eat chocolate.

Largest Rice Cake

Photo: Guinness World Records Limited

In 2007, at the 12th World Rice Food Festival in Dongjin-gun, Chungnam, South Korea, a rice cake was presented weighing 8,113 lb. (3.68 metric tons) and measuring 12 ft. 2 in. (3.7 m) in diameter.

Did You Know?

In Korea, rice cake colors have meaning. A first-birthday rice cake is colorful like a rainbow.

ACTIVITIES

1. Find South Korea on a map. What is its capital?

   _____

2. What island nation is a neighbor to South Korea?

   _____

3. Two-thirds of the world's population eat rice every day. Color two-thirds of the picture.

Largest Hamburger Commercially Available

Photo: Guinness World Records Limited

At a restaurant in Southgate, Michigan, a hamburger on the menu weighs 185.5 lb. (84.14 kg) and is available for $499, including cheese, pickles, onion, and bacon.

Did You Know?

The ground beef used to make this burger weighed 200 lb. (90.72 kg) before baking.

CHECK THIS OUT!

Many restaurants serve hamburgers in different sizes. There are quarter-pound burgers and half-pound burgers, but none of these comes close to the one that Mike Matkin made. His record hamburger weighed 185.5 pounds, about as much as a grown man! The burger is on the menu at Mallie's restaurant, but if you want to buy one, it'll cost you almost $500!

How do you make a burger this big? First, Mallie's sculpts the meat into a patty. Second, it takes three men to lift it into the oven. The burger cooks for 16 hours, and then must cool for 8 hours. Next, it's covered with toppings and placed on a huge bun. To order this burger, you must give Mallie's a 72-hour notice.

ACTIVITIES

1. In this passage, the word *sculpts* means:

   a. shapes

   b. grinds

   c. cooks

   d. elevates

2. Mallie's giant burger is wasteful. Do you agree with this statement? Explain why or why not.

   _____

   _____

3. How many quarter-pound burgers could be made from the 200 pounds of ground beef used in the world's Largest Hamburger Commercially Available? Circle your answer.

   800   400   600

4. If you owned a restaurant, what unusual item would you put on the menu to attract customers? Explain why you think your item would bring in business.

   _____

   _____

   _____

5. Finish the sentence.

   To order this burger, you must give Mallie's _____ .

6. Would you want to order the world's Largest Hamburger Commercially Available? Explain why or why not.

   _____

   _____

   _____

Largest Ice Cream Boat

Photo: Guinness World Records Limited

On April 18, 2004, in Stockholm, Sweden, the largest ice cream boat was displayed and weighed 1,910.3 lb. (866.5 kg).

Did You Know?

President George Washington loved ice cream. Records show that he spent about $200 on ice cream during the summer of 1790.

ACTIVITIES

1. If a coach bought $1.25 ice cream cones for 10 players, how much would he spend?

_____

2. Ask five people to tell their favorite flavor of ice cream. Color spaces in the graph to show your results.

vanilla					
chocolate					
cookie dough					
other					

Largest Potato Dumpling

Photo: Guinness World Records Limited

The 804.69 lb. (365 kg) potato dumpling was created on May 1, 2010, in Jena, Germany.

Did You Know?
In October 1995, the potato became the first vegetable to be grown in space.

ACTIVITIES

1. Have you ever been called "dumpling"? Other food-related terms of endearment are "sweet pea" and "honey." Write nicknames your family calls you.

_____

2. Circle your favorite kinds of soup.

tomato	chicken noodle	vegetable
minestrone	beef stew	egg drop
French onion	gumbo	potato

Most Jelly Eaten With Chopsticks in One Minute

Photo: Guinness World Records Limited

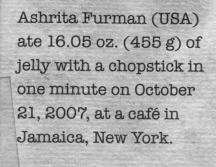

Ashrita Furman (USA) ate 16.05 oz. (455 g) of jelly with a chopstick in one minute on October 21, 2007, at a café in Jamaica, New York.

Did You Know?

The first chopsticks were made in China about 5,000 years ago and were probably twigs used to get hot food out of cooking pots.

ACTIVITIES

1. Try using a fork to eat soup or a table knife to eat peas. Describe your experience.

   _____

2. Some people love peanut butter and jelly, but to others it can be dangerous. Does someone at your school have a peanut allergy? What can you do to help keep him or her safe?

   _____

Largest Bowl of Pasta

Photo: Guinness World Records Limited

On March 12, 2010, a California restaurant made a bowl of pasta that weighed 13,786 lb. (6,253 kg). The pasta filled a portable pool that was 15 ft. (4.57 m) in diameter and 42 in. (106.7 cm) high. The pasta was covered with 10 gal. (37.85 L) of tomato sauce.

Did You Know?
Pasta comes in more than 600 shapes!

ACTIVITIES

1. Would you like to swim in a pool full of spaghetti? Why or why not?

   _____

2. If a gallon of pasta sauce costs $4.25, how much would eight gallons cost?

   _____

3. Diameter is the distance across a circle. What is the diameter in inches of the largest bowl in your kitchen?

   _____

Most Pizza Rolls Across the Shoulder in 30 Seconds

Photo: Guinness World Records Limited

On April 20, 2006, Tony Gemignani (USA) rolled a 20 oz. (567 g) ball of dough across his shoulders 37 times in 30 seconds during the filming of *Guinness World Records Week* on the Food Network channel.

Did You Know?

People from Brazil often choose green peas for their pizza topping. In Russia, they prefer a topping of mixed fishes and onions.

ACTIVITIES

1. How many times can you roll a ball across your shoulders?

   _____

2. How many more ounces would make the ball of dough weigh two pounds?

   _____

3. Can your pet do tricks? Do you have a special talent? Gather performers for an "Amazing Records" video or live performance. Write about your show.

   _____

   _____

Largest Haystack

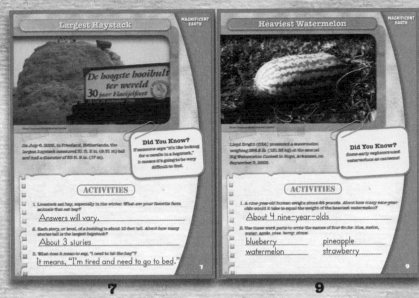

De hoogste hooibult ter wereld
30 jaar Flaeijelfeest

On July 6, 2005, in Friesland, Netherlands, the largest haystack measured 20 ft. 2 in. (6.21 m) tall and had a diameter of 55 ft. 9 in. (17 m).

Did You Know?
If someone says "it's like looking for a needle in a haystack," it means it's going to be very difficult to find.

ACTIVITIES

1. Livestock eat hay, especially in the winter. What are your favorite farm animals that eat hay?
   Answers will vary.

2. Each story, or level, of a building is about 10 feet tall. About how many stories tall is the largest haystack?
   About 3 stories

3. What does it mean to say, "I need to hit the hay"?
   It means, "I'm tired and need to go to bed."

7

Heaviest Watermelon

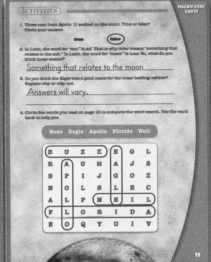

Lloyd Bright (USA) presented a watermelon weighing 268.8 lb. (121.93 kg) at the annual Big Watermelon Contest in Hope, Arkansas, on September 3, 2005.

Did You Know?
Some early explorers used watermelons as canteens!

ACTIVITIES

1. A nine-year-old human weighs about 65 pounds. About how many nine-year-olds would it take to equal the weight of the heaviest watermelon?
   About 4 nine-year-olds

2. Use these word parts to write the names of four fruits: blue, melon, water, apple, pine, berry, straw.
   blueberry   pineapple
   watermelon   strawberry

9

ACTIVITIES

1. Three men from Apollo 11 walked on the moon. True or false? Circle your answer.
   true   (false)

2. In Latin, the word for "sun" is sol. That is why solar means "something that relates to the sun." In Latin, the word for "moon" is luna. So, what do you think lunar means?
   Something that relates to the moon

3. Do you think the Eagle was a good name for the lunar landing vehicle? Explain why or why not.
   Answers will vary.

4. Circle five words you read on page 10 to complete the word search. Use the word bank to help you.

Buzz   Eagle   Apollo   Florida   Neil

B	U	Z	Z	E	G	L
E	A	U	H	A	J	S
B	P	I	J	G	O	Z
N	O	L	S	L	E	C
A	L	P	N	E	I	L
F	L	O	R	I	D	A
E	O	Q	Y	U	I	V

11

Greatest Mountain Range on Earth

The Himalayas were formed between 30 and 50 million years ago. They contain some of the 10 tallest peaks, including Mount Everest, the tallest mountain in the world.

Did You Know?
About 4,000 people have tried to climb to Mt. Everest's peak. Only 660 have made it so far.

ACTIVITIES

1. What mountain range is closest to your home?
   Answers will vary.

2. Would you rather climb a mountain or explore a cave? Why?
   Answers will vary.

3. Mt. Everest is 29,035 ft. tall. The second tallest mountain, called K2, is 28,251 feet tall. How many feet taller is Mt. Everest?
   778 feet taller

14

Heaviest Avocado

Gabriel Ramirez Nahim (Venezuela) presented an avocado that weighed 4 lb. 13 oz. (2.19 kg) on January 28, 2009.

Did You Know?
Another name for the avocado is the Alligator Pear, because of its shape and its green skin.

ACTIVITIES

1. Avocados are the main ingredient in guacamole. What words can you make from the letters G-U-A-C-A-M-O-L-E? Suggested answers:
   mole   game   male
   came   gum   camel

2. A single tree can produce about one picture box of avocados each year. How much could one tree produce in 4.5 years?
   2,250 avocados

15

ACTIVITIES

1. Why do you think Olympis took until July 30 to melt completely?
   Answers will vary.

2. Draw a picture of what you think Olympis looked like as she started to melt.

   Drawings will vary.

3. What are eight adjectives you could use to describe Olympis? Suggested answers:
   tall   unusual
   cold   record-breaking
   big   giant
   white   unique

4. Imagine you are building a snowman the size of Olympis. What supplies would you need?
   Answers will vary.

5. One ton is equal to 2,000 pounds. Olympis weighed 13,000,000 pounds. How many tons is that? Research to find out how much a typical car weighs. Did Olympis weigh more or less than a car?
   6,500 tons; less than a car

17

Largest Stone Sculpture

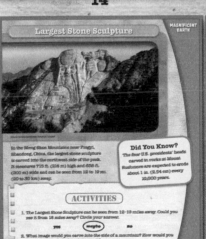

In the Meng Shan Mountains near Fangji, Shandong, China, the largest stone sculpture is carved into the mountain side of the peak. It measures 715 ft. (218 m) high and 656 ft. (200 m) wide and can be seen from 12 to 19 mi. (20 to 30 km) away.

Did You Know?
The four U.S. presidents' heads carved in rocks at Mount Rushmore are expected to erode about 1 in. (2.54 cm) every 10,000 years.

ACTIVITIES

1. The Largest Stone Sculpture can be seen from 12-19 miles away. Could you see it from 16 miles away? Circle your answer.
   yes   (maybe)   no

2. What image would you carve into the side of a mountain? How would you want people to feel when they saw it?
   Answers will vary.

3. What four U.S. presidents can be seen at Mount Rushmore?
   George Washington   Theodore Roosevelt
   Thomas Jefferson   Abraham Lincoln

19

ACTIVITIES

1. Which of the following words express the weight of the black diamond?
   a. fifty-five thousand five hundred fifty-five
   (b.) five hundred fifty-five and fifty-five hundredths
   c. five hundred fifty-five and fifty-five tenths
   d. fifty-five hundred and fifty-five hundredths

2. How many more facets does the world's Smallest Brilliant Cut Diamond have than the world's Largest Cut Diamond?
   2 facets

3. The gem cutter worked on the world's Smallest Brilliant Cut Diamond for ____ years.
   (a.) 2
   b. 5
   c. 10
   d. 15

4. People often wear diamonds in jewelry, such as rings or earrings. Do you own a special piece of jewelry? Why is it meaningful to you?
   Answers will vary.

5. The world's Largest Cut Diamond is black, but diamonds can also come in green. The world's Largest Green Diamond is 40.7 carats. About how many of the largest green diamonds would equal the weight of the Largest Cut Diamond? Fill in the chart to help you.

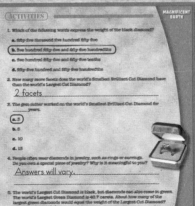

Number of Green Diamonds: About 14 green diamonds

23

Slowest Flowering Plant

The giant bromeliad was discovered in the Bolivian mountains in 1870. Its flower cluster emerges after about 80 to 150 years of the plant's life. Once it has blossomed, the plant dies.

Did You Know?
This plant is part of the pineapple family. When it blooms, as many as 8,000 flowers may open on a single spike.

ACTIVITIES

1. Giant bromeliads take about 115 years to bloom. If one is planted today, in what year is it likely to bloom?
   Answers will vary.

2. On average, humans live for about 78 years. Do giant bromeliads live longer or shorter than humans? Circle your answer.
   shorter   (longer)

3. What is your favorite plant or flower?
   Answers will vary.

26

ACTIVITIES

1. What does ingredient mean?
   Ingredient means a component or something that enters
   as an element into a mixture; Answers will vary.

2. Name three ingredients in your favorite food. Answers will vary.

3. Draw a picture to illustrate the expression, "When life gives you lemons, make lemonade."

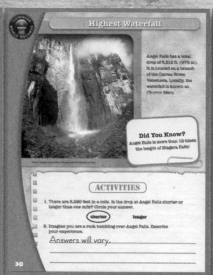

Drawings will vary.

4. In the passage on page 28, the word relieve means:
   a. strengthen
   b. identify
   c. **help** *(circled)*
   d. harm

5. Do you like the flavor of lemon? Explain why or why not.
   Answers will vary.

6. Make your own recipe for lemonade. How many lemons would you use? How much water and sugar? Share your lemonade with your family. Do they like it?
   Answers will vary.
   Lemons: _____ Water: _____ Sugar: _____

29

Highest Waterfall

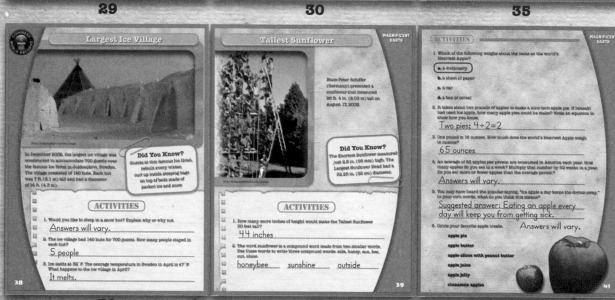

Angel Falls has a total drop of 3,212 ft. (979 m). It is located on a branch of the Carrao River, Venezuela. Locally, the waterfall is known as Churun Meru.

Did You Know?
Angel Falls is more than 12 times the height of Niagara Falls!

ACTIVITIES

1. There are 5,280 feet in a mile. Is the drop at Angel Falls shorter or longer than one mile? Circle your answer.
   shorter *(circled)*   longer

2. Imagine you are a rock tumbling over Angel Falls. Describe your experience.
   Answers will vary.

30

ACTIVITIES

1. Some people think that a four-leaf clover is a sign of:
   a. love
   b. faith
   c. **luck** *(circled)*
   d. hope

2. Sir John Melton wrote about finding "some good thing." Write about some good thing that you have found.
   Answers will vary.

3. Think about the meaning people have given to each leaf of a four-leaf clover: faith, hope, love, and luck. If you found a five-leaf clover, what meaning would you give the fifth leaf? Explain your answer.
   Answers will vary.

4. An 18-leaf clover is about the size of how many four-leaf clovers put together?
   4½ four-leaf clovers

5. The year 1620 was how many years ago?
   Answers will vary depending on the current year.

6. Draw your own 18-leaf clover.

   Drawings will vary.

35

Largest Ice Village

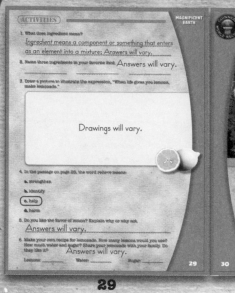

In December 2008, the largest ice village was constructed to accommodate 700 guests near the famous Ice Hotel in Jukkasjärvi, Sweden. The village consisted of 140 huts. Each hut was 7 ft. (2.1 m) tall and had a diameter of 14 ft. (4.3 m).

Did You Know?
Guests at this famous Ice Hotel, rebuilt every winter, curl up inside sleeping bags on top of beds made of packed ice and snow.

ACTIVITIES

1. Would you like to sleep in a snow hut? Explain why or why not.
   Answers will vary.

2. The ice village had 140 huts for 700 guests. How many people stayed in each hut?
   5 people

3. Ice melts at 32° F. The average temperature in Sweden in April is 41° F. What happens to the ice village in April?
   It melts.

38

Tallest Sunflower

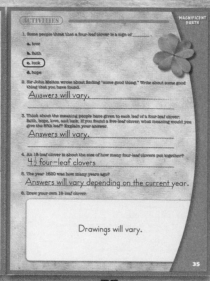

Hans-Peter Schiffer (Germany) presented a sunflower that measured 26 ft. 4 in. (8.03 m) tall on August 17, 2009.

Did You Know?
The Shortest Sunflower measured just 2.2 in. (56 mm) high. The Largest Sunflower Head had a 32.25 in. (82 cm) diameter.

ACTIVITIES

1. How many more inches of height would make the Tallest Sunflower 30 feet tall?
   44 inches

2. The word sunflower is a compound word made from two smaller words. Use these words to write three compound words: side, honey, sun, bee, out, shine.
   honeybee   sunshine   outside

39

ACTIVITIES

1. Which of the following weighs about the same as the world's Heaviest Apple?
   a. **a dictionary** *(circled)*
   b. a sheet of paper
   c. a car
   d. a box of cereal

2. It takes about two pounds of apples to make a nine-inch apple pie. If Donald had used his apple, how many apple pies could he make? Write an equation to show how you know.
   Two pies; 4÷2=2

3. One pound is 16 ounces. How much does the world's Heaviest Apple weigh in ounces?
   65 ounces

4. An average of 65 apples per person are consumed in America each year. How many apples do you eat in a week? Multiply that number by 52 weeks in a year. Do you eat more or fewer apples than the average person?
   Answers will vary.

5. You may have heard the popular saying, "An apple a day keeps the doctor away." In your own words, what do you think this means?
   Suggested answer: Eating an apple every
   day will keep you from getting sick.

6. Circle your favorite apple treats.   Answers will vary.
   apple pie
   apple butter
   apple slices with peanut butter
   apple juice
   apple jelly
   cinnamon apples

41

Longest-Lasting Lightning Storm

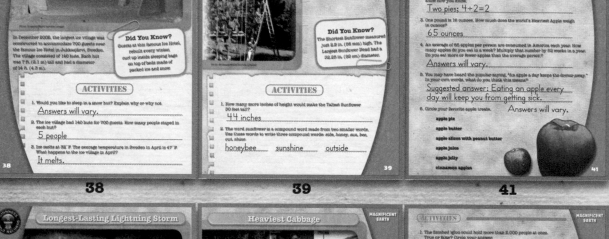

The longest-lasting lightning storm raged in Saturn's upper atmosphere for more than eight months in 2009. The storm made lightning bolts that were about 10,000 times stronger than those on Earth.

Did You Know?
A bolt of lightning can stretch more than five miles long, and can contain 100 million volts of electricity!

ACTIVITIES

1. Eight months is what fraction of a year?
   ⅔ of a year

2. What planet is sixth from the sun in our solar system?
   Saturn

3. What two planets are closest to Earth?
   Venus   Mars

42

Heaviest Cabbage

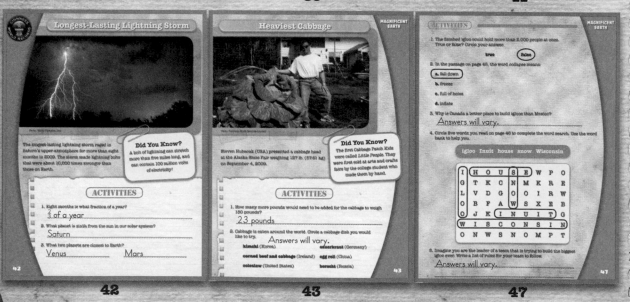

Steven Hubacek (USA) presented a cabbage head at the Alaska State Fair weighing 127 lb. (57.61 kg) on September 4, 2009.

Did You Know?
The first Cabbage Patch Kids were called Little People. They were first sold at arts and crafts fairs by the college student who made them by hand.

ACTIVITIES

1. How many more pounds would need to be added for the cabbage to weigh 150 pounds?
   23 pounds

2. Cabbage is eaten around the world. Circle a cabbage dish you would like to try.   Answers will vary.
   kimchi (Korea)   sauerkraut (Germany)
   corned beef and cabbage (Ireland)   egg roll (China)
   coleslaw (United States)   borscht (Russia)

43

ACTIVITIES

1. The finished igloo could hold more than 5,000 people at once. True or false? Circle your answer.
   true   **false** *(circled)*

2. In the passage on page 46, the word collapse means:
   a. **fall down** *(circled)*
   b. freeze
   c. full of holes
   d. inflate

3. Why is Canada a better place to build igloos than Mexico?
   Answers will vary.

4. Circle five words you read on page 46 to complete the word search. Use the word bank to help you.

   igloo Inuit house snow Wisconsin

   ```
   I  H  O  U  S  E  W  P  O
   G  T  K  C  N  M  K  R  E
   L  V  D  G  O  O  I  R  W
   O  B  F  A  W  S  X  E  B
   J  K  I  N  U  I  T  G
   W  I  S  C  O  N  S  I  N
   O  N  W  S  N  O  M  P  T
   ```

5. Imagine you are the leader of a team that is trying to build the biggest igloo ever. Write a list of rules for your team to follow.
   Answers will vary.

47

Most Electricity Generated by Pedaling on Bicycles for 24 Hours

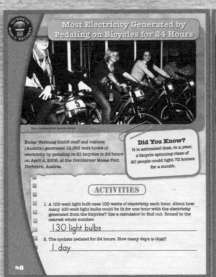

Ender Werbung GmbH staff and visitors (Austria) generated 12,963 watt hours of electricity by pedaling on 21 bicycles in 24 hours on April 4, 2006, at the Dornbirner Messe Fair, Dornbirn, Austria.

Did You Know?
It is estimated that, in a year, a bicycle spinning class of 20 people could light 72 homes for a month.

ACTIVITIES

1. A 100-watt light bulb uses 100 watts of electricity each hour. About how many 100-watt light bulbs could be lit for one hour with the electricity generated from the bicycles? Use a calculator to find out. Round to the nearest whole number.
130 light bulbs

2. The cyclists pedaled for 24 hours. How many days is that?
1 day

48

Heaviest Sweet Potato

On March 8, 2004, Manuel Pérez Pérez (Spain) presented a sweet potato that weighed 81 lb. 9 oz. (37 kg).

Did You Know?
Sweet potatoes are not potatoes! They are part of the morning glory family, a flowering vine.

ACTIVITIES

1. How many more ounces would make the Heaviest Sweet Potato weigh 82 pounds?
7 ounces

2. How many groups of 9 are in 81?
9

3. Sweet potatoes are often eaten at Thanksgiving. What is your favorite Thanksgiving food?
Answers will vary.

49

Tallest Zinnia

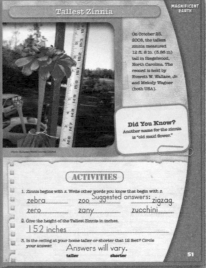

On October 23, 2008, the tallest zinnia measured 12 ft. 8 in. (3.86 m) tall in Napierwood, North Carolina. The record is held by Everett W. Wallace, Jr. and Melody Wagner (both USA).

Did You Know?
Another name for the zinnia is "old maid flower."

ACTIVITIES

1. Zinnia begins with z. Write other words you know that begin with z.
zebra   zoo   Suggested answers: zigzag
zero   zany   zucchini

2. Give the height of the Tallest Zinnia in inches.
152 inches

3. Is the ceiling at your home taller or shorter than 12 feet? Circle your answer. **Answers will vary.**
taller   shorter

51

ACTIVITIES

1. The largest trees in the world are the
a. redwood trees.
b. red oak trees.
c. birch trees.
d. cherry trees

2. The giant sequoia General Sherman is found in California. True or false? Circle your answer.
true   false

3. Design a birdhouse that you think would be suitable to hang on General Sherman. Draw it here.

Drawings will vary.

4. General Sherman is 271 feet tall. How tall are you? In inches, how much taller is General Sherman?
Answers will vary.

5. Imagine standing at the base of General Sherman and looking up toward its uppermost branches. Write a paragraph describing how you would feel.
Answers will vary.

53

Greatest Snowfall for a Single Snowstorm

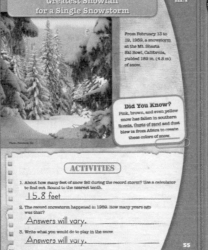

From February 13 to 19, 1959, a snowstorm at the Mt. Shasta Ski Bowl, California, yielded 189 in. (4.8 m) of snow.

Did You Know?
Pink, brown, and even yellow snow has fallen in southern Russia. Gusts of sand and dust blew in from Africa to create these colors of snow.

ACTIVITIES

1. About how many feet of snow fell during the record storm? Use a calculator to find out. Round to the nearest tenth.
15.8 feet

2. The record snowstorm happened in 1959. How many years ago was that?
Answers will vary.

3. Write what you would do to play in the snow.
Answers will vary.

55

Heaviest Squash

On September 21, 2007, Bradley Wursten (Netherlands) presented a squash that weighed 1,234 lb. (559.75 kg).

Did You Know?
Many flowers can be eaten and are sometimes added to stir-fry dishes, pancake batter, or salads. Squash blossoms are sometimes dipped in batter and fried.

ACTIVITIES

1. Does the heaviest squash weigh more or less than one ton? Circle your answer.
less than one ton   more than one ton

2. How many more pounds would make the squash weigh 1,500 pounds?
266 pounds

3. The word squash can be a noun and a verb. Write a definition for each.
squash (n.): **a fleshy fruit related to pumpkins**
squash (v.): **to press or crush**

56

Largest Tree Transplanted

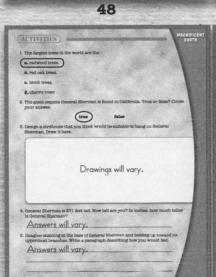

Old Glory measured 58 ft. (17.67 m) tall, 104 ft. (31.6 m) wide, and weighed approximately 916,000 lb. (415.5 metric tons) when it was transplanted on January 20, 2004. It was between 180 and 220 years old.

Did You Know?
This oak tree was moved because of a road-widening project, at a cost of $1 million!

ACTIVITIES

1. This tree was named Old Glory. What other object is commonly called Old Glory?
The U.S. flag

2. Old Glory is an oak tree. Which one is the oak leaf? Color it.

57

ACTIVITIES

1. Is the circumference of the snowball closer to 21 feet or 22 feet? Circle your answer.
21 feet   22 feet

2. How much larger is the new record snowball than the old record snowball? Write an equation to show how you know.
4 feet, 6 inches; 21 feet, 3 inches − 16 feet, 9 inches = 4 feet, 6 inches

3. Which of the following faces would you see if the world's Largest Snowball were cut top to bottom and separated?
a.
b.
c.
d.

4. A ball is a spherical body or shape. What is another definition of ball?
Suggested answer: A large formal party featuring dancing

5. Three-thousand seven-hundred forty-five people gathered together to set this world record. What was the last thing you did as part of a group? Did you enjoy it? Explain why or why not.
Answers will vary.

59

Largest Cucumber Plant

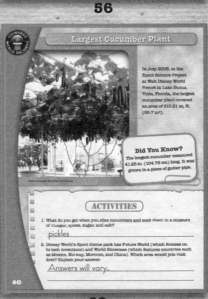

In July 2008, at the Epcot Science Project at Walt Disney World Resort in Lake Buena Vista, Florida, the largest cucumber plant covered an area of 610.31 sq. ft. (56.7 m²).

Did You Know?
The longest cucumber measured 41.25 in. (104.78 cm) long. It was grown in a piece of gutter pipe.

ACTIVITIES

1. What do you get when you slice cucumbers and soak them in a mixture of vinegar, spices, sugar, and salt?
pickles

2. Disney World's Epcot theme park has Future World (which focuses on hi-tech inventions) and World Showcase (which features countries such as Mexico, Norway, Morocco, and China). Which area would you visit first? Explain your answer.
Answers will vary.

60

Largest Permanent Hedge Maze

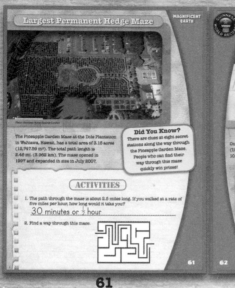

The Pineapple Garden Maze at the Dole Plantation in Wahiawa, Hawaii, has a total area of 3.15 acres (12,747.59 m²). The total path length is 2.46 mi. (3.962 km). The maze opened in 1997 and expanded in size in July 2007.

Did You Know?
There are clues at eight secret stations along the way through the Pineapple Garden Maze. People who can find their way through this maze quickly win prizes!

ACTIVITIES

1. The path through the maze is about 2.5 miles long. If you walked at a rate of five miles per hour, how long would it take you?
   30 minutes or ½ hour

2. Find a way through this maze.

61

Heaviest Pepper

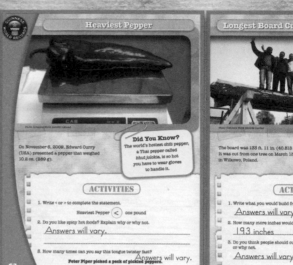

On November 6, 2009, Edward Curry (USA) presented a pepper that weighed 10.2 oz. (289 g).

Did You Know?
The world's hottest chili pepper, a Thai pepper called bhut jolokia, is so hot you have to wear gloves to handle it.

ACTIVITIES

1. Write < or > to complete the statement.
   Heaviest Pepper < one pound

2. Do you like spicy hot foods? Explain why or why not.
   Answers will vary.

3. How many times can you say this tongue twister fast?
   Answers will vary.
   Peter Piper picked a peck of pickled peppers.

62

Longest Board Cut From One Tree

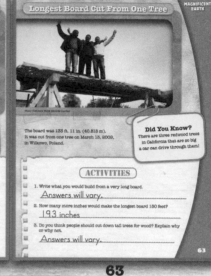

The board was 133 ft. 11 in. (40.815 m). It was cut from one tree on March 13, 2009, in Wilkowo, Poland.

Did You Know?
There are three redwood trees in California that are so big a car can drive through them!

ACTIVITIES

1. Write what you would build from a very long board.
   Answers will vary.

2. How many more inches would make the longest board 150 feet?
   193 inches

3. Do you think people should cut down tall trees for wood? Explain why or why not.
   Answers will vary.

63

Fastest Growing Plant

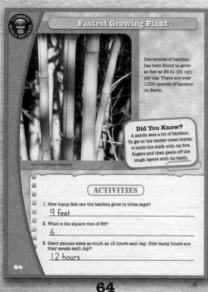

One species of bamboo has been found to grow as fast as 36 in. (91 cm) per day. There are over 1,000 species of bamboo on Earth.

Did You Know?
A panda eats a lot of bamboo. To get to the tender meat inside, it holds the stalk with its five fingers and then peels off the tough layers with its teeth.

ACTIVITIES

1. How many feet can the bamboo grow in three days?
   9 feet

2. What is the square root of 36?
   6

3. Giant pandas sleep as much as 12 hours each day. How many hours are they awake each day?
   12 hours

64

Most Participants in a Snowboard Race

A snowboard race with 88 participants was held in Christchurch, New Zealand, on October 6, 2007.

Did You Know?
Snowboarding is one of the fastest growing sports in the U.S. It became a Winter Olympic Sport in 1998.

ACTIVITIES

1. If one snowboarder launched every 30 seconds, how many minutes would it take 88 snowboarders to launch?
   44 minutes

2. What country is New Zealand's closest neighbor?
   Australia

3. Would you rather ride a surfboard, a skateboard, or a snowboard? Explain why.
   Answers will vary.

67

Most People Carving Pumpkins Simultaneously

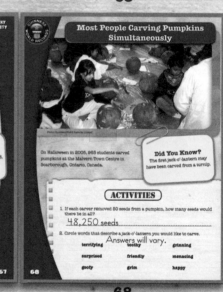

On Halloween in 2005, 965 students carved pumpkins at the Malvern Town Centre in Scarborough, Ontario, Canada.

Did You Know?
The first jack-o'-lantern may have been carved from a turnip.

ACTIVITIES

1. If each carver removed 50 seeds from a pumpkin, how many seeds would there be in all?
   48,250 seeds

2. Circle words that describe a jack-o'-lantern you would like to carve.
   Answers will vary.

   terrifying   toothy   grinning
   surprised   friendly   menacing
   goofy   grim   happy

68

Largest Human Wheelbarrow Race

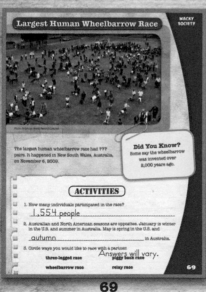

The largest human wheelbarrow race had 777 pairs. It happened in New South Wales, Australia, on November 6, 2009.

Did You Know?
Some say the wheelbarrow was invented over 2,000 years ago.

ACTIVITIES

1. How many individuals participated in the race?
   1,554 people

2. Australian and North American seasons are opposite. January is winter in the U.S. and summer in Australia. May is spring in the U.S. and _autumn_ in Australia.

3. Circle ways you would like to race with a partner.
   Answers will vary.

   three-legged race   piggy back race
   wheelbarrow race   relay race

69

ACTIVITIES

1. What is a daredevil? What are some pros and cons of being a daredevil?
   A recklessly daring person;
   Answers will vary.

2. The people who set the record for the most people on one moving motorcycle are from
   a. India
   b. USA
   c. China
   d. Japan

3. Circle five words you read on page 70 to complete the word search. Use the word bank to help you.

   Evel   motorcycle   India   fractures   jumps

L	O	P	T	E	V	E	L	K	Q
M	O	T	O	R	C	Y	C	L	E
E	P	I	M	N	C	X	W	A	S
K	O	N	J	U	M	P	S	U	D
H	A	D	O	K	J	H	N	B	V
E	W	I	O	L	U	C	E	A	S
F	R	A	C	T	U	R	E	S	L
R	D	E	S	C	Z	G	T	Y	I

4. The "Tornadoes" Army Service Corps Motorcycle Display Team rode a single motorcycle 0.68 miles. How long does it take you to run that far? Ask an adult to time you.
   Answers will vary.

71

Longest Chain of People Licking Lollipops

A chain of 12,831 people licked lollipops on September 7, 2008, in Valladolid, Spain.

Did You Know?
National Lollipop Day is celebrated in the U.S. on July 20th.

ACTIVITIES

1. If 30 people could stand in each row, how many rows would be needed for all the lollipop-lickers? Round to the nearest whole number.
   428 rows

2. If 5,000 people chose a cherry lollipop, how many chose some other flavor?
   7,831

3. What is your favorite lollipop flavor?
   Answers will vary.

73

Most People Folding T-Shirts

On May 14, 2009, at a shopping center in London, United Kingdom, 275 people folded T-shirts at the same time.

Did You Know?
T-shirts were once worn only as underwear. James Dean shocked people by wearing one in the 1955 movie *Rebel Without a Cause.*

ACTIVITIES

1. If one person took 9.5 seconds to fold a shirt, one took 11 seconds, one took 12 seconds, and one took 14.5 seconds, what was the average time it took to fold a shirt?
   11.75 seconds

2. If each member of your family wears one shirt each day, how many shirts are worn in two weeks?
   Answers will vary.

3. Write what you do to help with the laundry.
   Answers will vary.

74

Most People Dribbling Basketballs at the Same Time

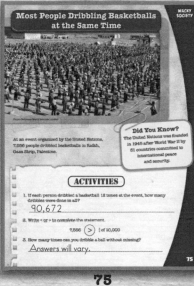

At an event organized by the United Nations, 7,556 people dribbled basketballs in Rafah, Gaza Strip, Palestine.

Did You Know?
The United Nations was founded in 1945 after World War II by 51 countries committed to international peace and security.

ACTIVITIES

1. If each person dribbled a basketball 12 times at the event, how many dribbles were done in all?
   90,672

2. Write < or > to complete the statement.
   7,556 $>$ 10,000

3. How many times can you dribble a ball without missing?
   Answers will vary.

75

ACTIVITIES

1. How many people were buried in the sand for this world record?
   a. 480
   b. 517
   c. 500
   d. 37

2. Unscramble words you read on page 76.
   hacbe — **beach**
   lvestifa — **festival**
   dasn — **sand**
   stanovcsis — **vacations**
   danssctslen — **sandcastles**

3. Have you been to the beach? If so, what did you like about it? If you have not visited the beach, would you like to? Explain why or why not.
   Answers will vary.

4. Circle things you could do at the beach.
   swim
   ski
   surf
   build sandcastles
   relax
   make snow angels

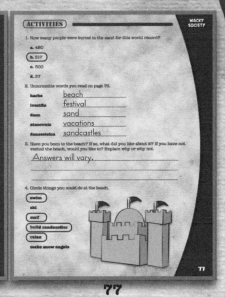

77

Most People Twirling Batons

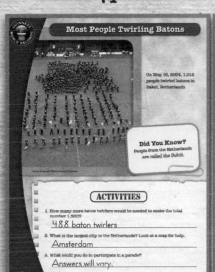

On May 16, 2004, 1,012 people twirled batons in Bakel, Netherlands.

Did You Know?
People from the Netherlands are called the Dutch.

ACTIVITIES

1. How many more baton twirlers would be needed to make the total number 1,500?
   488 baton twirlers

2. What is the largest city in the Netherlands? Look at a map for help.
   Amsterdam

3. What could you do to participate in a parade?
   Answers will vary.

78

Most Custard Pies Thrown by Two Teams of 10

The largest custard pie fight involved 3,320 pies thrown by two teams of 10 in three minutes in Bolton, United Kingdom, in 2005.

Did You Know?
A famous pie fight can be seen in the 1941 Three Stooges comedy *Slim In the Sweet Pie and Pie.*

ACTIVITIES

1. Twenty people threw 3,320 pies. How many pies did each person throw?
   166 pies

2. The pie fight lasted for three minutes. About how many pies were thrown each minute? Round to the nearest whole number.
   1,107 pies

3. Would you rather throw a pie or get "pied"? Explain why.
   Answers will vary.

79

Largest Game of Simon Says

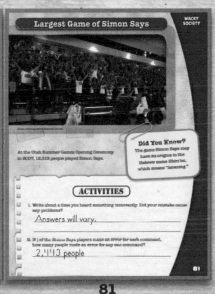

At the Utah Summer Games Opening Ceremony in 2007, 12,219 people played Simon Says.

Did You Know?
The game Simon Says may have its origins in the Hebrew name *Shim'on,* which means "listening."

ACTIVITIES

1. Write about a time you heard something incorrectly. Did your mistake cause any problems?
   Answers will vary.

2. If ½ of the Simon Says players made an error for each command, how many people made an error for any one command?
   2,113 people

81

ACTIVITIES

1. Pepperoni is said to be the most popular pizza topping. What is your favorite topping? Explain why.
   Answers will vary.

2. If 95% of your class at school has eaten pizza in the last month, about how many students have not eaten pizza in that time frame?
   Answers will vary.

3. Unscramble words you read on page 82.
   cnba — **bacon**
   ionon — **onions**
   vohcaenei — **anchovies**
   smuohorm — **mushrooms**
   segusa — **sausage**
   prpeponi — **pepperoni**
   negre repppes — **green peppers**

4. Why do you think Super Bowl Sunday is a popular day to order pizza?
   Answers will vary.

5. If three billion pizzas are sold each year, about how many are sold per day? Round to the nearest whole number.
   About 8,219,178 pizzas

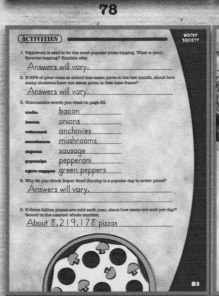

83

Largest Simultaneous Yo-Yo

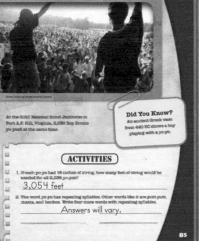

At the 2010 National Scout Jamboree in Fort A.P. Hill, Virginia, 2,036 Boy Scouts yo-yoed at the same time.

Did You Know?
An ancient Greek vase from 440 BC shows a boy playing with a yo-yo.

ACTIVITIES

1. If each yo-yo had 18 inches of string, how many feet of string would be needed for all 2,036 yo-yos?
   3,054 feet

2. The word yo-yo has repeating syllables. Other words like it are putt-putt, mama, and bonbon. Write four more words with repeating syllables.
   Answers will vary.

85

Largest "YMCA" Dance

At an event organized by the Sun Bowl Association in Texas, 40,148 people did the "YMCA" dance on December 31, 2008.

Did You Know?
YMCA stands for "Young Men's Christian Association." It was founded in 1844 by George Williams in London, England.

ACTIVITIES

1. What letters other than Y-M-C-A can you form with your body? Use your body to spell words for a friend to guess. Take turns. What was the most difficult word to guess?
   Answers will vary.

2. The record was set in a stadium. If the stadium had 16 sections, about how many people could sit in each section? Use a calculator to find out. Round to the nearest whole number.
   2,509 people

86

Largest Gathering of People Dressed as Superman

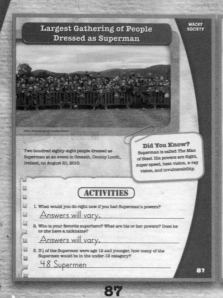

Two hundred eighty-eight people dressed as Superman at an event in Omeath, County Louth, Ireland, on August 21, 2010.

Did You Know?
Superman is called The Man of Steel. His powers are flight, super speed, heat vision, x-ray vision, and invulnerability.

ACTIVITIES

1. What would you do right now if you had Superman's powers?
   Answers will vary.

2. Who is your favorite superhero? What are his or her powers? Does he or she have a nickname?
   Answers will vary.

3. If ⅓ of the Supermen were age 12 and younger, how many of the Supermen would be in the under-12 category?
   48 Supermen

87

---

1. Name four ways participants were invited to the multi-legged race.
   online   brochures
   through social networking   word-of-mouth

2. If 305 people were involved in a race, how many legs were there in all?
   610 legs

3. What does unison mean? Write your own sentence using that word.
   Acting simultaneously;
   Answers will vary.

4. Circle five words you read on page 88 to complete the word search. Use the word bank to help you.

race   ankles   teamwork   runners   partner

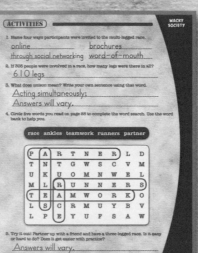

P	A	R	T	N	E	R	L	D
T	N	T	G	W	S	C	V	M
K	U	O	M	N	W	E	L	
M	L	R	U	N	N	E	R	S
T	E	A	M	W	O	R	K	O
L	S	C	R	M	U	Y	B	V
L	P	E	Y	U	F	S	A	W

5. Try it out! Partner up with a friend and have a three-legged race. Is it easy or hard to do? Does it get easier with practice?
   Answers will vary.

89

Largest Easter Egg Hunt

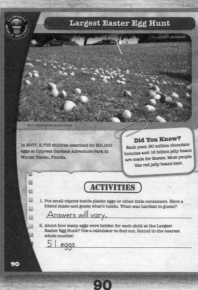

In 2007, 9,753 children searched for 501,000 eggs at Cypress Gardens Adventure Park in Winter Haven, Florida.

Did You Know?
Each year, 90 million chocolate bunnies and 16 billion jelly beans are made for Easter. Most people like red jelly beans best.

ACTIVITIES

1. Put small objects inside plastic eggs or other little containers. Have a friend shake and guess what's inside. What was hardest to guess?
   Answers will vary.

2. About how many eggs were hidden for each child at the Largest Easter Egg Hunt? Use a calculator to find out. Round to the nearest whole number.
   51 eggs

90

Largest Tea Party

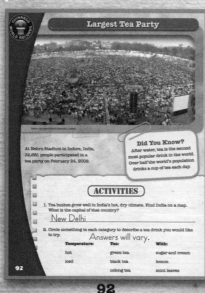

At Nehru Stadium in Indore, India, 32,681 people participated in a tea party on February 24, 2008.

Did You Know?
After water, tea is the second most popular drink in the world. Over half the world's population drinks a cup of tea each day.

ACTIVITIES

1. Tea bushes grow well in India's hot, dry climate. Find India on a map. What is the capital of that country?
   New Delhi

2. Circle something in each category to describe a tea drink you would like to try.
   Answers will vary.

Temperature:	Tea:	With:
hot	green tea	sugar and cream
iced	black tea	lemon
	oolong tea	mint leaves

92

Largest Dog Walk (Single Breed)

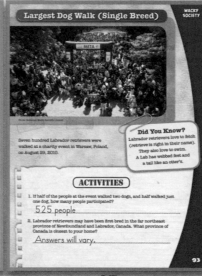

Seven hundred Labrador retrievers were walked at a charity event in Warsaw, Poland, on August 29, 2010.

Did You Know?
Labrador retrievers love to fetch (retrieve is right in their name). They also love to swim. A Lab has webbed feet and a tail like an otter's.

ACTIVITIES

1. If half of the people at the event walked two dogs, and half walked just one dog, how many people participated?
   525 people

2. Labrador retrievers may have been first bred in the far northeast province of Newfoundland and Labrador, Canada. What province of Canada is closest to your home?
   Answers will vary.

93

---

1. How many bananas does the average American eat per year?
   a. 2 pounds
   b. 7 pounds
   c. 27 pounds
   d. 72 pounds

2. How many banana varieties are grown in the world? Circle your answer.
   more than 300   more than 1,500

3. Finish the sentence.
   Bananas are a good source of vitamin B6.

4. Conduct an experiment! Take two unripe bananas. Put one in the refrigerator and leave one on the counter. Observe the bananas for one week. What happens to both bananas?
   Answers will vary.

5. What is your favorite fruit? With an adult, make a smoothie using a banana, your favorite fruit, and some milk or yogurt. List the ingredients you used.
   Answers will vary.

6. Find a map of the world. Where is London? What direction is London from where you live?
   Answers will vary.

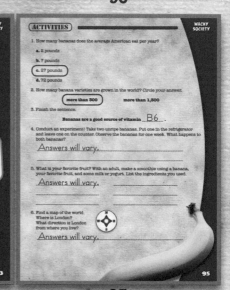

95

Longest Marathon Playing Dodgeball

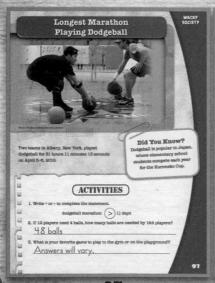

Two teams in Albany, New York, played dodgeball for 31 hours 11 minutes 13 seconds on April 5–6, 2010.

Did You Know?
Dodgeball is popular in Japan, where elementary school students compete each year for the Kuroneko Cup.

ACTIVITIES

1. Write < or > to complete the statement.
   dodgeball marathon (>) 1½ days

2. If 12 players need 4 balls, how many balls are needed by 144 players?
   48 balls

3. What is your favorite game to play in the gym or on the playground?
   Answers will vary.

97

Most People Brushing Their Teeth

On November 5, 2005, 13,380 people brushed their teeth at the Cuscatlán Stadium in the city of San Salvador in El Salvador.

Did You Know?
Sharks lose teeth throughout their lives. Whenever they lose a tooth, a new one grows to take its place.

ACTIVITIES

1. If each brusher at the stadium spit three times, what was the total number of spits?
   40,140 spits

2. If a tube of toothpaste lasts for 36 brushes and you brush twice a day, in how many days will you need a new tube?
   18 days

3. List four things you do to keep your teeth healthy.
   Answers will vary.

98

Largest Gathering of Elvis Impersonators

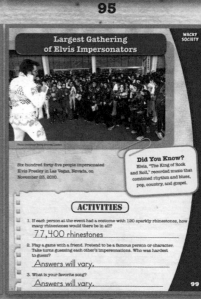

Six hundred forty-five people impersonated Elvis Presley in Las Vegas, Nevada, on November 23, 2010.

Did You Know?
Elvis, "The King of Rock and Roll," recorded music that combined rhythm and blues, pop, country, and gospel.

ACTIVITIES

1. If each person at the event had a costume with 120 sparkly rhinestones, how many rhinestones would there be in all?
   77,400 rhinestones

2. Play a game with a friend. Pretend to be a famous person or character. Take turns guessing each other's impersonations. Who was hardest to guess?
   Answers will vary.

3. What is your favorite song?
   Answers will vary.

99

101

ACTIVITIES

WACKY SOCIETY

1. Apples are grown in all 50 states. How many states can you identify in 60 seconds? Ask an adult to time you. Color the states that you can identify correctly.

Answers will vary.

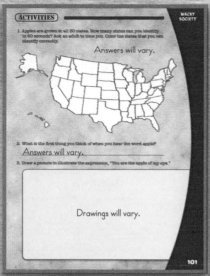

2. What is the first thing you think of when you hear the word apple?

Answers will vary.

3. Draw a picture to illustrate the expression, "You are the apple of my eye."

Drawings will vary.

101

102

Largest Tug-of-War Tournament

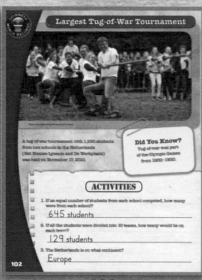

A tug-of-war tournament with 1,290 students from two schools in the Netherlands (Het Nieuwe Lyceum and De Werkplaats) was held on November 17, 2010.

Did You Know?
Tug-of-war was part of the Olympic Games from 1900-1920.

ACTIVITIES

1. If an equal number of students from each school competed, how many were from each school?

645 students

2. If all the students were divided into 10 teams, how many would be on each team?

129 students

3. The Netherlands is on what continent?

Europe

102

103

Most People Crammed in a Smart Car

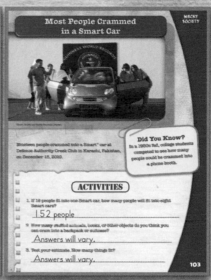

Nineteen people crammed into a Smart car at Defence Authority Creek Club in Karachi, Pakistan, on December 15, 2010.

Did You Know?
In a 1950s fad, college students competed to see how many people could be crammed into a phone booth.

ACTIVITIES

1. If 19 people fit into one Smart car, how many people will fit into eight Smart cars?

152 people

2. How many stuffed animals, books, or other objects do you think you can cram into a backpack or suitcase?

Answers will vary.

3. Test your estimate. How many things fit?

Answers will vary.

103

104

Most People Keeping a Soccer Ball in the Air

In Yong City, China, 1,062 students and fans at Yanshan University kept soccer balls in the air on July 30, 2010.

Did You Know?
The participants controlled the soccer balls in the air for 11 seconds.

ACTIVITIES

1. If the participants stood in 18 rows, how many people would be in each row?

59 people

2. For how many seconds can you keep a ball or a balloon in the air?

Answers will vary.

3. What type of ball do you control best?

Answers will vary.

104

107

ACTIVITIES

WACKY SOCIETY

Complete the crossword puzzle with words you read on page 106.

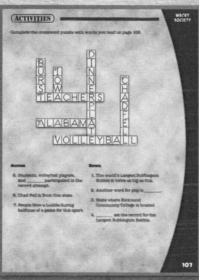

Across

5. Students, volleyball players, and _____ participated in the record attempt.

6. Chad Fell is from this state.

7. People blow a bubble during halftime of a game for this sport.

Down

1. The world's Largest Bubblegum Bubble is twice as big as this.

2. Another word for pop is _____.

3. State where Kirkwood Community College is located.

4. _____ set the record for the Largest Bubblegum Bubble.

107

108

Most People Arm Wrestling

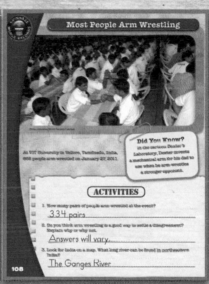

At VIT University in Vellore, Tamilnadu, India, 668 people arm-wrestled on January 29, 2011.

Did You Know?
In the cartoon Dexter's Laboratory, Dexter invents a mechanical arm for his dad to use when he arm-wrestles a stronger opponent.

ACTIVITIES

1. How many pairs of people arm-wrestled at the event?

334 pairs

2. Do you think arm wrestling is a good way to settle a disagreement? Explain why or why not.

Answers will vary.

3. Look for India on a map. What long river can be found in northeastern India?

The Ganges River

108

110

Most People Wearing Wigs (Single Venue)

At a National Hockey League game in Philadelphia, Pennsylvania, 9,315 people wore wigs on October 30, 2005.

Did You Know?
In ancient Egypt, men and women wore wigs of human hair, wool, or fibers. The more elaborate the wig, the higher the social status.

ACTIVITIES

1. If every third person at the event wore an orange wig, how many orange wigs would there be?

3,105 orange wigs

2. Draw a wacky wig on this head.

Drawings will vary.

110

111

Most People Dressed as Smurfs

At Swansea University in Swansea, United Kingdom, 2,510 people dressed as Smurfs on June 8, 2009.

Did You Know?
Smurfs were created by Belgian cartoonist Peyo. He invented the word smurf when he couldn't remember the word he wanted to say.

ACTIVITIES

1. How many groups of 10 Smurfs were at the event?

251 groups

2. In Smurf language, smurf can be any part of speech. For example, if you woke up in a bad mood, you could say, "I just smurfed up and I'm feeling smurfy." Write a sentence in which smurf or another silly word is used as a noun, a verb, and an adjective.

Answers will vary.

111

113

ACTIVITIES

WACKY SOCIETY

1. The high five may have been born in 1977. How many years ago was that? Circle your answer.

(more than 30)   less than 30

2. How many people set the record for Most People Doing Chest Bumps?

a. 666
b. 123
c. 290
(d. 433)

3. Are you part of a team? What is your role on the team?

Answers will vary.

4. Look at a map of Australia. How many states and mainland territories does it have? Fill in the blanks below.

6 states   2 mainland territories

5. Now, do some research about Australia. What is the capital? What are some animals found in Australia? Would you want to visit Australia?

The capital of Australia is Canberra. Australian animals include the koala, wombat, kangaroo, and dingo. Answers will vary.

6. What are the meanings of these Australian slang words?

G'day: hello   Rug Rat: child
Sheila: female   Croc: crocodile
Bloke: male   Uni: university

113

Most People Crammed on an Unmodified Bus

Did You Know?

ACTIVITIES

1. The record is for an unmodified bus. What could be modified, or changed, in a bus to allow more people to fit?

Answers will vary.

2. If each seat on the bus could hold six people, about how many seats would be needed? Round to the nearest whole number.

35 seats

3. Look at a map. What large country is west of Poland?

Germany

114

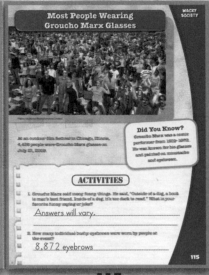

Most People Wearing Groucho Marx Glasses

Did You Know?

ACTIVITIES

1. Groucho Marx said many funny things. He said, "Outside of a dog, a book is man's best friend. Inside of a dog, it's too dark to read." What is your favorite funny saying or joke?

Answers will vary.

2. How many individual bushy eyebrows were worn by people at the event?

8,872 eyebrows

115

Most People Spinning Tops Simultaneously

Did You Know?

ACTIVITIES

1. If each person at the event spin a top three times, how many spins were completed in all?

1,131 spins

2. Playing with a top lets you explore how things move in our universe. Potential energy change to kinetic energy when you spin a top. Momentum keeps the top spinning perfectly for a while. What happens as energy begins to lessen?

The top slows down and wobbles, then drops.

116

---

114   115   116

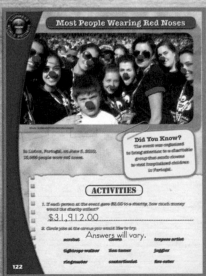

ACTIVITIES

1. What does scuba stand for?

a. Self-Contained Underwater Breathing Apparatus

b. Self-Contained Underwater Breathing Device

c. Super Cool Underwater Breathing Adventure

d. Self-Contained Maximum Breathing Apparatus

2. Finish the sentence.

Indonesia is often referred to as the world's largest archipelago

3. Draw a picture of what you might see while scuba diving.

Drawings will vary.

4. Look up a picture of the Indonesian flag. Draw it here.

119

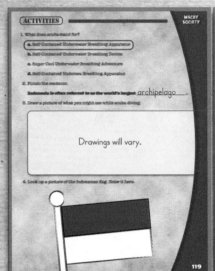

Most People Balancing Books on Their Heads

Did You Know?

ACTIVITIES

1. If ⅔ of the people at the event were male, how many were female?

626 people were female

2. How good is your sense of balance? Stand on one leg with your eyes closed. For how many seconds can you hold it?

Answers will vary.

3. For how many seconds can you balance this book on your head?

Answers will vary.

120

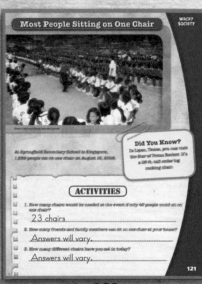

Most People Sitting on One Chair

Did You Know?

ACTIVITIES

1. How many chairs would be needed at the event if only 48 people could sit on one chair?

23 chairs

2. How many friends and family members can sit on one chair at your house?

Answers will vary.

3. How many different chairs have you sat in today?

Answers will vary.

121

---

119   120   121

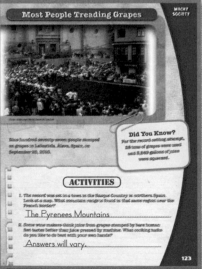

Most People Wearing Red Noses

Did You Know?

ACTIVITIES

1. If each person at the event gave $2.00 to a charity, how much money would the charity collect?

$31,912.00

2. Circle jobs at the circus you would like to try. Answers will vary.

acrobat   trapeze artist

tightrope walker   lion tamer   juggler

ringmaster   contortionist   fire eater

122

Most People Treading Grapes

Did You Know?

ACTIVITIES

1. The record was set in a town in the Basque Country in northern Spain. Look at a map. What mountain range is found in that same region near the French border?

The Pyrenees Mountains

2. Some wine makers think juice from grapes stamped by bare human feet tastes better than juice pressed by machine. What cooking tasks do you like to do best with your own hands?

Answers will vary.

123

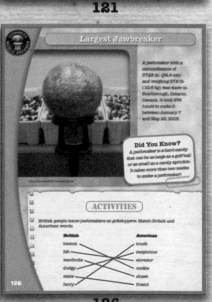

Largest Jawbreaker

Did You Know?

ACTIVITIES

1. British people know jawbreakers as gobstoppers. Match British and American words.

British	American
tissue	truck
lift	suspicious
wardrobe	elevator
dodgy	cookie
mate	closet
lorry	friend

126

---

122   123   126

127

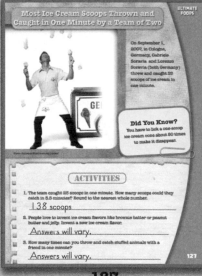

Most Ice Cream Scoops Thrown and Caught in One Minute by a Team of Two

ULTIMATE FOODS

ACTIVITIES

1. The team caught 25 scoops in one minute. How many scoops could they catch in 5.5 minutes? Round to the nearest whole number.

138 scoops

2. People love to invent ice cream flavors like brownie batter or peanut butter and jelly. Invent a new ice cream flavor.

Answers will vary.

3. How many times can you throw and catch stuffed animals with a friend in one minute?

Answers will vary.

127

128

Largest Curry

ULTIMATE FOODS

ACTIVITIES

1. Curry is a mix of meat and vegetables in a spicy sauce. What is your favorite spicy food?

Answers will vary.

2. Many people in India love curry. Look at a map. What large mountain range is north of India?

The Himalaya Mountains

3. The largest curry weighed 22,707 pounds. What number is in the hundreds place?

7

128

129

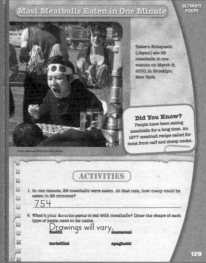

Most Meatballs Eaten in One Minute

ULTIMATE FOODS

ACTIVITIES

1. In one minute, 29 meatballs were eaten. At that rate, how many could be eaten in 26 minutes?

754

2. What's your favorite pasta to eat with meatballs? Draw the shape of each type of pasta next to its name.

Drawings will vary.

fusilli   macaroni

tortellini   spaghetti

129

131

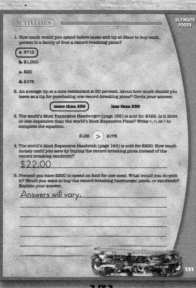

ACTIVITIES

ULTIMATE FOODS

1. How much would you spend before taxes and tip at Maze to buy each person in a family of four a record-breaking pizza?

a. $713
b. $1,000
c. $20
d. $178

2. An average tip at a nice restaurant is 20 percent. About how much should you leave as a tip for purchasing one record-breaking pizza? Circle your answer.

more than $30   less than $30

3. The world's Most Expensive Hamburger (page 168) is sold for $160. Is it more or less expensive than the world's Most Expensive Pizza? Write <, >, or = to complete the equation.

$168 > $178

4. The world's Most Expensive Sandwich (page 144) is sold for $200. How much money could you save by buying the record-breaking pizza instead of the record-breaking sandwich?

$22.00

5. Pretend you have $200 to spend on food for one meal. What would you do with it? Would you want to buy the record-breaking hamburger, pizza, or sandwich? Explain your answer.

Answers will vary.

131

132

Largest Scrambled Eggs

ULTIMATE FOODS

On December 1, 2009, scrambled eggs weighing 2,755 lb. 11 oz. (1,240 kg) were made in Cathedral Square, Christchurch, New Zealand. More than 20,000 eggs and 26.4 gal. (100 L) of cream were used to make the eggs.

Did You Know?
A chicken farm in Ohio has 4.6 million hens that lay about 3.7 million eggs—every day!

ACTIVITIES

1. How do you like to eat eggs for breakfast?

Answers will vary.

2. About 20,000 eggs were used for this record. What is ⅒ of 20,000?

2,000

3. If a gallon of cream costs $10, how much would 26.5 gallons of cream cost?

$265.00

132

135

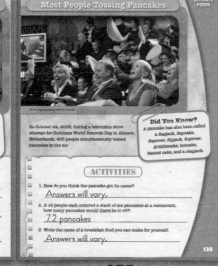

Most People Tossing Pancakes

ULTIMATE FOODS

On October 24, 2008, during a television show attempt for Guinness World Records Day in Almere, Netherlands, 405 people simultaneously tossed pancakes in the air.

Did You Know?
A pancake has also been called a flapjack, flapcake, flapover, flipjack, flopover, griddlecake, hotcake, flannel cake, and a slapjack.

ACTIVITIES

1. How do you think the pancake got its name?

Answers will vary.

2. If 12 people each ordered a stack of six pancakes at a restaurant, how many pancakes would there be in all?

72 pancakes

3. Write the name of a breakfast food you can make for yourself.

Answers will vary.

135

137

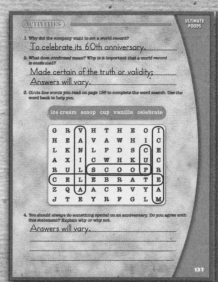

ACTIVITIES

ULTIMATE FOODS

1. Why did the company want to set a world record?

To celebrate its 60th anniversary.

2. What does confirmed mean? Why is it important that a world record is confirmed?

Made certain of the truth or validity;
Answers will vary.

3. Circle five words you read on page 136 to complete the word search. Use the word bank to help you.

ice cream   scoop   cup   vanilla   celebrate

G	R	V	H	T	H	E	O	I	
H	E	A	V	A	W	H	I	C	
L	K	N	L	P	D	S	C	E	
A	X	I	C	W	H	K	U	C	
R	U	L	S	C	O	O	P	R	
C	E	L	E	B	R	A	T	E	
Z	Q	A	A	C	R	V	Y	A	
J	T	E	Y	R	F	G	L	M	

4. You should always do something special on an anniversary. Do you agree with this statement? Explain why or why not.

Answers will vary.

137

138

Longest Line of Pizzas

ULTIMATE FOODS

On May 16, 2009, the Van Dozer Foundation and the St. Lucie County Education Foundation (both USA) assembled a 1,777 ft. 7 in. (541.8 m) line of 12 in. (30.48 cm) pizzas. It took 1,800 pizzas to make the line in Fort Pierce, Florida.

Did You Know?
A pizza made in Madrid, Spain, was hand-delivered 12,347 mi. (19,870 km) away in Wellington, New Zealand.

ACTIVITIES

1. What number is in the thousands place in 1,800?

1

2. Draw lines to divide these pizzas so that five people can each have four slices. Suggested answer:

138

139

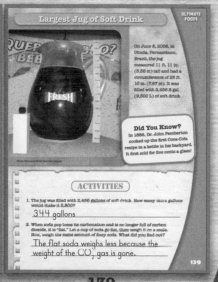

Largest Jug of Soft Drink

ULTIMATE FOODS

On June 6, 2006, in Olinda, Pernambuco, Brazil, the jug measured 11 ft. 11 in. (3.36 m) tall and had a circumference of 25 ft. 10 in. (7.87 m). It was filled with 2,456.6 gal. (9,300 L) of soft drink.

Did You Know?
In 1886, Dr. John Pemberton cooked up the first Coca-Cola recipe in a kettle in his backyard. It first sold for five cents a glass!

ACTIVITIES

1. The jug was filled with 2,456 gallons of soft drink. How many more gallons would make it 2,800?

344 gallons

2. When soda pop loses its carbonation and is no longer full of carbon dioxide, it is "flat." Let a cup of soda go flat, then weigh it on a scale. Now, weigh the same amount of fizzy soda. What did you find out?

The flat soda weighs less because the weight of the CO_2 gas is gone.

139

Largest Pretzel

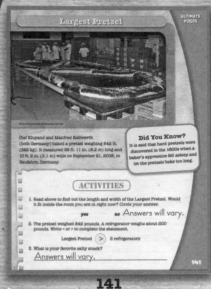

Olaf Klrjrand and Manfred Kellwerth (both Germany) baked a pretzel weighing 842 lb. (382 kg). It measured 26 ft. 11 in. (8.2 m) long and 10 ft. 2 in. (3.1 m) wide on September 21, 2008, in Beufabra, Germany.

Did You Know?
It is said that hard pretzels were discovered in the 1600s when a baker's apprentice fell asleep and let the pretzels bake too long.

ACTIVITIES

1. Read above to find out the length and width of the Largest Pretzel. Would it fit inside the room you are in right now? Circle your answer.

   yes   no   Answers will vary.

2. The pretzel weighed 842 pounds. A refrigerator weighs about 200 pounds. Write < or > to complete the statement.

   Largest Pretzel > 3 refrigerators

3. What is your favorite salty snack?
   Answers will vary.

141

ACTIVITIES

1. What is the radius of the pan in which the world's Largest Pancake was cooked?
   25 feet

2. Arrange these numbers in order from least to greatest.

   5,966.4   1,074.7   2,000,000   6,614

   1,074.7   5,966.4   6,614   2,000,000

3. The world's Largest Cinnamon Roll weighed 246.5 pounds. Which equation would you use to find how much more the world's Largest Pancake weighed than the world's Largest Cinnamon Roll? (Hint: n equals the difference in weight.)

   a. 6,614 ÷ n = 246.5
   b. 6,614 − 246.5 = n
   c. 246.5 ÷ n = 6,614
   d. 246.5 ÷ n = 6,614

4. What is the answer to the equation you chose in #3?
   n = 6,367.5

5. What do you usually eat for breakfast? What are some things you could change to make it healthier?
   Answers will vary.

6. What are some objects that are the same shape as a pancake? Draw them here.

   Drawings will vary.

143

Most Expensive Sandwich

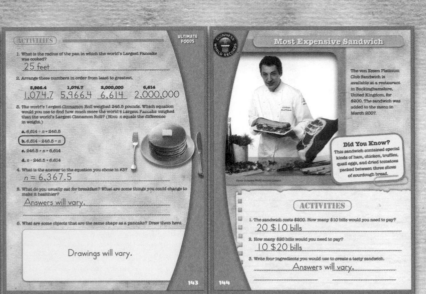

The von Essen Platinum Club Sandwich is available at a restaurant in Buckinghamshire, United Kingdom, for $200. The sandwich was added to the menu in March 2007.

Did You Know?
This sandwich contained special kinds of ham, chicken, truffles, quail eggs, and dried tomatoes packed between three slices of sourdough bread.

ACTIVITIES

1. The sandwich costs $200. How many $10 bills would you need to pay?
   20 $10 bills

2. How many $20 bills would you need to pay?
   10 $20 bills

3. Write four ingredients you would use to create a tasty sandwich.
   Answers will vary.

144

Fastest Time to Eat a 12-Inch Pizza

On March 22, 2008, Josh Anderson (New Zealand) ate a 12 in. (30.48 cm) pizza in 1 minute 45.37 seconds.

Did You Know?
The first mozzarella cheese was made from the milk of a water buffalo!

ACTIVITIES

1. Anderson ate one pizza in about 1½ minutes. About how many pizzas could he eat in five minutes? Round to the nearest whole number.
   About 3 pizzas

2. Circle your favorite pizza toppings.   Answers will vary.

   chicken   mushrooms   pepperoni
   pineapple   peppers   sausage
   onions   spinach   tomatoes

146

Largest Paella

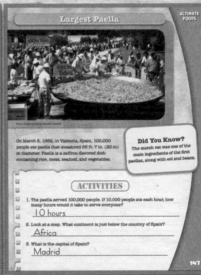

On March 8, 1992, in Valencia, Spain, 100,000 people ate paella that measured 65 ft. 7 in. (20 m) in diameter. Paella is a saffron-flavored dish containing rice, meat, seafood, and vegetables.

Did You Know?
The marsh rat was one of the main ingredients of the first paellas, along with eel and beans.

ACTIVITIES

1. The paella served 100,000 people. If 10,000 people ate each hour, how many hours would it take to serve everyone?
   10 hours

2. Look at a map. What continent is just below the country of Spain?
   Africa

3. What is the capital of Spain?
   Madrid

147

ACTIVITIES

1. Earthworms can be a good source of protein. Research different types of foods that provide protein for our bodies. Create a menu that features these food items. Include an appetizer, a main course, and a dessert.

   Menu
   Answers will vary.

2. What types of things has Manu eaten?

   a. squid, insects, and snakes
   b. frog legs, caviar, and snakes
   c. lizards, insects, and snakes
   d. squid, frog legs, and caviar

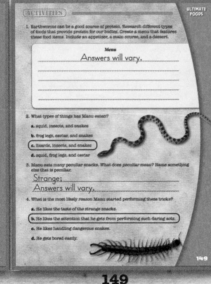

3. Manu eats many peculiar snacks. What does peculiar mean? Name something else that is peculiar.
   Strange;
   Answers will vary.

4. What is the most likely reason Manu started performing these tricks?

   a. He likes the taste of the strange snacks.
   b. He likes the attention that he gets from performing such daring acts.
   c. He likes handling dangerous snakes.
   d. He gets bored easily.

149

ACTIVITIES

1. Find Germany and South Africa on a map. On what continents are these two countries? About how many miles separate them?
   Germany is in Europe, and South Africa is in Africa; About 9,000 miles.

2. How do you eat a chocolate rabbit? One study found that 91 percent of Americans think you should eat the ears first. Do you agree? Explain why or why not.
   Answers will vary.

3. Chocolate rabbits have been around for 400 years. True or false? Circle your answer.
   true   false

4. Chocolate rabbits were originally made to celebrate spring. What other ways do people celebrate spring?
   Answers will vary.

5. Conduct a survey of your friends and family to find out their favorite kinds of chocolate. How many like dark chocolate best, how many like milk chocolate best, and how many like white chocolate best? How many do not like chocolate at all? Make a chart to display your results.

   Answers will vary.

155

Highest Dinner Party

On May 3, 2004, eight people, including an appointed butler, dined in formal clothing at 22,326 ft. (6,805 m) on Lhakpa Ri, Tibet.

Did You Know?
The food for this party included caviar, duck, chocolate bombe, cheese, and birthday cake.

ACTIVITIES

1. If you could have your next birthday party anywhere in the world, where would it be?
   Answers will vary.

2. If each table seats eight people, how many tables would 104 people need?
   13 tables

3. Who would you invite to a fancy dinner?
   Answers will vary.

156

Largest Popcorn Ball

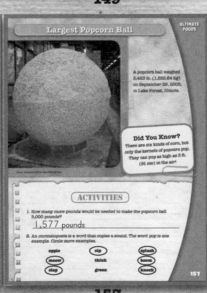

A popcorn ball weighed 3,423 lb. (1,552.54 kg) on September 29, 2006, in Lake Forest, Illinois.

Did You Know?
There are six kinds of corn, but only the kernels of popcorn pop. They can pop as high as 3 ft. (91 cm) in the air!

ACTIVITIES

1. How many more pounds would be needed to make the popcorn ball 5,000 pounds?
   1,577 pounds

2. An onomatopoeia is a word that copies a sound. The word pop is one example. Circle more examples.

   apple   zip   splash
   meow   think   boom
   clap   green   knock

157

Strangest Diet

Since 1966, Michel Lotito (France) has eaten 18 bicycles, 15 shopping carts, seven televisions, six chandeliers, two beds, a pair of skis, a Cessna light aircraft, and a computer. He first learned of his unusual ability when his drinking glass broke and he began chewing the pieces.

Did You Know?
Lotito can eat grocery carts and bicycles, but says that eating bananas and hard-boiled eggs makes him sick!

ACTIVITIES

1. How many wheels do 18 bicycles have?
   36 wheels

2. Do you love carrots or toast with jam? What food have you eaten three times or more in the past week?
   Answers will vary.

3. How many items did Lotito eat in all?
   52 items

158

Largest Serving of French Fries

On February 19, 2004, an 812.4 lb. (368.5 kg) bag of French fries was made at the Hereford Racecourse in Hereford, United Kingdom.

Did You Know?
During the Potato Bowl USA in 2005, about 10,000 people ate 4,621 lb. (2,096 kg) of French fries with 113 gal. (428 L) of ketchup.

ACTIVITIES

1. If one potato makes 15 French fries, how many fries could you make from six potatoes?
   90 French fries

2. With adult help, make healthy oven fries. Coat potato wedges with olive oil and some salt. Bake in a 400°F oven for 15-20 minutes. How did your fries taste?
   Answers will vary.

159

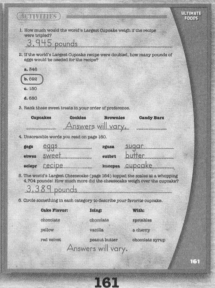

ACTIVITIES

1. How much would the world's Largest Cupcake weigh if the recipe were tripled?
   3,945 pounds

2. If the world's Largest Cupcake recipe were doubled, how many pounds of eggs would be needed for the recipe?
   a. 346
   b. 662
   c. 150
   d. 680

3. Rank these sweet treats in your order of preference.

Cupcakes	Cookies	Brownies	Candy Bars

   Answers will vary.

4. Unscramble words you read on page 160.

gegs	**eggs**	rgusa	**sugar**
etwss	**sweet**	eutbrt	**butter**
eciepr	**recipe**	kucepa	**cupcake**

5. The world's Largest Cheesecake (page 164) topped the scales at a whopping 4,704 pounds! How much more did the cheesecake weigh over the cupcake?
   3,389 pounds

6. Circle something in each category to describe your favorite cupcake.

Cake Flavor:	Icing:	With:
chocolate	chocolate	sprinkles
yellow	vanilla	a cherry
red velvet	peanut butter	chocolate syrup

   Answers will vary.

161

Largest Bag of Potato Chips

On March 11, 2004, the largest bag of potato chips was made in Bradford, West Yorkshire, United Kingdom. It weighed 113 lb. 7 oz. (51.35 kg).

Did You Know?
A couple hundred years ago, potatoes were served for dessert!

ACTIVITIES

1. How many more ounces of potato chips would be needed for a 115-pound bag?
   25 ounces

2. At $2.25 per bag, how much would three bags of chips cost?
   $6.75

3. Baked, mashed, or fried? What is your favorite way to eat potatoes?
   Answers will vary.

163

Largest Cheesecake

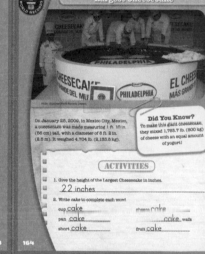

On January 25, 2009, in Mexico City, Mexico, a cheesecake was made measuring 1 ft. 10 in. (56 cm) tall, with a diameter of 8 ft. 2 in. (2.5 m). It weighed 4,704 lb. (2,133.5 kg).

Did You Know?
To make this giant cheesecake, they mixed 1,763.7 lb. (800 kg) of cheese with an equal amount of yogurt!

ACTIVITIES

1. Give the height of the Largest Cheesecake in inches.
   22 inches

2. Write cake to complete each word.

   cup**cake**   chees**cake**
   pan**cake**   **cake**walk
   short**cake**   fruit**cake**

164

Most Expensive Hamburger

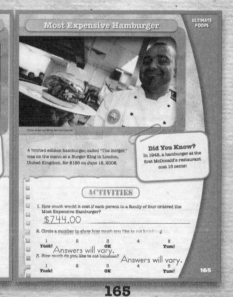

A limited-edition hamburger, called "The Burger," was on the menu at a Burger King in London, United Kingdom, for $186 on June 15, 2008.

Did You Know?
In 1948, a hamburger at the first McDonald's restaurant cost 15 cents!

ACTIVITIES

1. How much would it cost if each person in a family of four ordered the Most Expensive Hamburger?
   $744.00

2. Circle a number to show how much you like to eat hamburgers.
   Yuck! 1 2 3 OK 4 5 Yum!
   Answers will vary.

3. How much do you like to eat bananas?
   Yuck! 1 2 3 OK 4 5 Yum!
   Answers will vary.

165

ACTIVITIES

1. When did Bannister begin collecting banana items?
   a. 1972
   b. 1976
   c. 1927
   d. 1967

2. How many countries are represented in the International Banana Club? Circle your answer.
   more than 15   less than 15

3. What does quest mean? Write your own sentence using that word.
   A search in order to find something;
   Answers will vary.

4. Read the following statements. Circle true or false.

   Bannister is known as "Banana Kid."   true   **false**
   Anyone can join the Banana Club.   **true**   false
   The museum is in California.   **true**   false

5. Bannister designed his own sticker for the International Banana Club. Design and draw a sticker for a club that you create.

   Drawings will vary.

167

Largest Steak Commercially Available

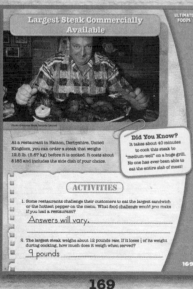

At a restaurant in Hatton, Derbyshire, United Kingdom, you can order a steak that weighs 12.5 lb. (5.67 kg) before it is cooked. It costs about $185 and includes the side dish of your choice.

Did You Know?
It takes about 40 minutes to cook this steak to "medium-well" on a huge grill. No one has ever been able to eat the entire slab of meat!

ACTIVITIES

1. Some restaurants challenge their customers to eat the largest sandwich or the hottest pepper on the menu. What food challenge would you make if you had a restaurant?
   Answers will vary.

2. The largest steak weighs about 12 pounds raw. If it loses ¼ of its weight during cooking, how much does it weigh when served?
   9 pounds

169

Largest Hot Cross Bun

The largest hot cross bun was made on April 4, 2009, in Capetown, South Africa, and weighed 227.08 lb. (103 kg).

Did You Know?
A grandmother in the United Kingdom owns a hot cross bun that was baked in 1821, nearly 200 years ago!

ACTIVITIES

1. Does the largest Hot Cross Bun weigh more or less than the Largest Bag of Potato Chips on page 163? Circle your answer.
   more   less

2. Sharing a hot cross bun is said to bond friends, especially if they say, "Half for you and half for me, between us two shall goodwill be." Write what you shared with a friend.
   Answers will vary.

170

Largest Prawn/Shrimp Cocktail

On July 10, 2009, in London, United Kingdom, a 219.54 lb. (99.72 kg) glass of shrimp cocktail was served in a cocktail glass that measured 4 ft. 11 in. (1.5 m) tall.

Did You Know?
A shrimp's head is half of its body size, and its heart is located in its head!

ACTIVITIES

1. If you need 1½ dozen shrimp for a recipe, how many shrimp should you buy?
18 shrimp

2. Ask five people to tell their favorite kind of seafood. Color spaces in the graph to show your results. **Answers will vary.**

fish	
shrimp	
crab	
lobster	

171

171

ACTIVITIES

ULTIMATE FOODS

1. How many seconds are there in two minutes?
a. 60
b. 90
c. 120
d. 150

2. If one ordinary pizza weighs 12.7 pounds, about how many ordinary pizzas would it take to equal the weight of the world's Largest Pizza?
About 9,953 pizzas

3. Complete the crossword puzzle with words you read on page 172.

Across
2. The world's Largest Pizza used 9,920 pounds of _____.
4. The world's Largest Pizza used 3,968 pounds of _____.
5. A _____ pizza is usually 16 inches in diameter.
6. The world's Largest Pizza was made here.
7. Place where you can order a pizza for dinner

Down
1. He holds the record for the Largest Pizza Base Spun in Two Minutes.
3. State where Tony Gemignani set his world record

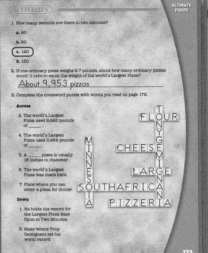

FLOUR
TONYGEMIGNANI
CHEESE
MINNESOTA
LARGE
SOUTHAFRICA
PIZZERIA

173

173

Largest Potato Gratin

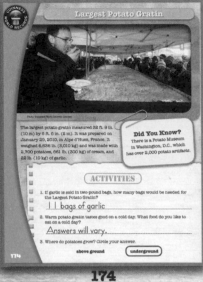

The largest potato gratin measured 32 ft. 9 in. (10 m) by 6 ft. 6 in. (2 m). It was prepared on January 29, 2010, in Alpe d'Huez, France. It weighed 6,636 lb. (3,010 kg) and was made with 2,700 potatoes, 661 lb. (300 kg) of cream, and 22 lb. (10 kg) of garlic.

Did You Know?
There is a Potato Museum in Washington, D.C. which has over 2,000 potato artifacts.

ACTIVITIES

1. If garlic is sold in two-pound bags, how many bags would be needed for the Largest Potato Gratin?
11 bags of garlic

2. Warm potato gratin tastes good on a cold day. What food do you like to eat on a cold day?
Answers will vary.

3. Where do potatoes grow? Circle your answer.
above ground   **underground**

174

174

Fastest Time to Eat a Bowl of Pasta

On November 18, 2009, Ernesto Cesario (Italy) ate a bowl of pasta in 1 minute 30 seconds. The pasta and sauce weighed 5.3 oz. (150 g).

Did You Know?
President Thomas Jefferson bought a machine for making macaroni in Italy and helped to make macaroni and cheese famous in the United States.

ACTIVITIES

1. How many seconds did it take Cesario to eat the bowl of pasta?
90 seconds

2. Did the bowl of pasta weigh more or less than ½ pound? Circle your answer.
more   **less**

3. What is your favorite kind of pasta sauce?
Answers will vary.

175

175

Largest Rice Cake

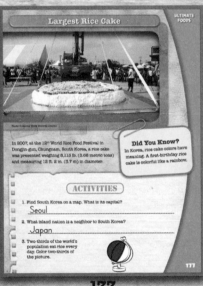

In 2007, at the 12th World Rice Food Festival in Dongjin-gun, Chungnam, South Korea, a rice cake was presented weighing 8,113 lb. (3.68 metric tons) and measuring 12 ft. 2 in. (3.7 m) in diameter.

Did You Know?
In Korea, rice cake colors have meaning. A first-birthday rice cake is colorful like a rainbow.

ACTIVITIES

1. Find South Korea on a map. What is its capital?
Seoul

2. What island nation is a neighbor to South Korea?
Japan

3. Two-thirds of the world's population eat rice every day. Color two-thirds of the picture.

177

177

ACTIVITIES

ULTIMATE FOODS

1. In this passage, the word sculpts means:
a. shapes
b. grinds
c. cooks
d. elevates

2. Mallie's giant burger is wasteful. Do you agree with this statement? Explain why or why not.
Answers will vary.

3. How many quarter-pound burgers could be made from the 200 pounds of ground beef used in the world's Largest Hamburger Commercially Available? Circle your answer.
800   400   600

4. If you owned a restaurant, what unusual item would you put on the menu to attract customers? Explain why you think your item would bring in business.
Answers will vary.

5. Finish the sentence.
To order this burger, you must give Mallie's **a 72-hour notice**

6. Would you want to order the world's Largest Hamburger Commercially Available? Explain why or why not.
Answers will vary.

179

179

Largest Ice Cream Boat

On April 18, 2004, in Stockholm, Sweden, the largest ice cream boat was displayed and weighed 1,910.5 lb. (866.5 kg).

Did You Know?
President George Washington loved ice cream. Records show that he spent about $200 on ice cream during the summer of 1790.

ACTIVITIES

1. If a coach bought $1.25 ice cream cones for 10 players, how much would he spend?
$12.50

2. Ask five people to tell their favorite flavor of ice cream. Color spaces in the graph to show your results. **Answers will vary.**

vanilla	
chocolate	
cookie dough	
other	

180

180

Largest Bowl of Pasta

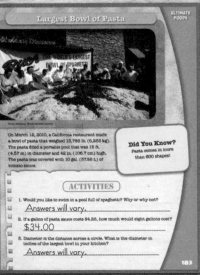

On March 12, 2010, a California restaurant made a bowl of pasta that weighed 13,780 lb. (6,253 kg). The pasta filled a portable pool that was 15 ft. (4.57 m) in diameter and 42 in. (106.7 cm) high. The pasta was covered with 10 gal. (37.86 L) of tomato sauce.

Did You Know?
Pasta comes in more than 600 shapes!

ACTIVITIES

1. Would you like to swim in a pool full of spaghetti? Why or why not?
Answers will vary.

2. If a gallon of pasta sauce costs $4.25, how much would eight gallons cost?
$34.00

3. Diameter is the distance across a circle. What is the diameter in inches of the largest bowl in your kitchen?
Answers will vary.

183

183

Most Pizza Rolls Across the Shoulder in 30 Seconds

On April 20, 2006, Tony Gemignani (USA) rolled a 20 oz. (567 g) ball of dough across his shoulders 37 times in 30 seconds during the filming of Guinness World Records Week on the Food Network channel.

Did You Know?
People from Brazil often choose green peas for their pizza topping. In Russia, they prefer a topping of mixed fishes and onions.

ACTIVITIES

1. How many times can you roll a ball across your shoulders?
Answers will vary.

2. How many more ounces would make the ball of dough weigh two pounds?
12 ounces

3. Can your pet do tricks? Do you have a special talent? Gather performers for an "Amazing Records" video or live performance. Write about your show.
Answers will vary.

184

184